The Universal Mind

Beyond Human Experience

TOM J. LIMBER

Two Center Publishing

JACKSONVILLE, FLORIDA

Published by:
Two Center Publishing
PO Box 54032, Jacksonville, FL 32246
http://two.center/

Cover design by Tom J. Limber
Back cover photo by Allison Meyer

ISBN-10: 0-692-91886-8
ISBN-13: 978-0-692-91886-9
Library of Congress Control Number: 2017912826

Limber, Tom J. The Universal Mind. 1st ed., vol. 1, Two Center Publishing, 2017.

Printed in the United States of America

First Edition

Dedicated to Allison

CONTENTS

ACKNOWLEDGMENTS

Allison for her belief in me and continued support.

Father Thomas Jr., mother Rosemary, and stepfather Dave, my sister Lorrie, and grandparents Raymond & Mariam Dunn, in addition to Thomas Sr. & Louise.

Chad, Shelia, Jace and Chase for a lifetime of friendship.

Jeremy, Sara, and Willa for your friendship and advice.

Elizabeth Gotski for professional editing and review.

Thank you to the many mentors and students I have had over the years because your expertise has been invaluable.

INTRODUCTION

It is true that life on Earth could greatly be enhanced by the encounters we have with others on a subjective level. This is primarily from an attempt to understand other cultures, ways of life, and personalities. As humans, we continuously learn and find that those around us inspire a positive energy which leads to self-discovery through some form of communication. This ultimately gives us a sense of certainty in ourselves and our progress. This association with self-understanding reminds us of our determination. However, some people feel uncertain or disconnected from the world and lack the purpose of an outlook about the future.

Many people do not have the personal interest or motivation that they may have once had in their life. As a human gets older, they lose the ambition to improve their quality of life. The reason for this is mostly because of exhaustion, but also sometimes out of a fear of failure. This also depends on the amount of people involved in the activity, as the will to move forward is only present in those who put forth the time and effort to make the event happen. However, in other people that are not completely focused on success, the subjective mind does not encompass goals, and those that are lacking in this drive tend to be set back when they should be moving forward.

This book is meant to ease the problem of uncertainty in the mind by ensuring that a true purpose is developed and transformed over time to a concrete view that can be used to follow a natural path to certainty, deduction, and true living as far as civilization is concerned.

This book is a path; it is an arrangement of enhanced independent thought, which focuses on the subjective mind. As we progress on our journey, we will analyze key interests and long-term objectives that help us understand the internal nature of our mind. All with the purpose of finding internal, personal origins of the self to show that a mind can become 'universal' by following three specific concepts: Theory, Action, and Change. These concepts are also known to be 'realities' or ways of discerning memories and change through action. These comprise the necessary factors of human understanding, which all equate to a symbolic method which will be covered later in this text.

It is my hope that you will develop your own internal philosophy from the concepts outlined and use those ideas to expand upon the nature of who you are in this life and, most importantly, what you want to be. When you move forward with any mental based philosophical system, you will encounter symbols. In this case, the text starts as a visual construct in the mind, but then as you progress with the methods outlined, a network of ideas starts to emerge, and from there, we find the 'universal' mind. It can be agreed upon by most that it is impossible to totally understand the nature of our reality due to its extreme complexity and 'busy' nature, but through this system of thought, we use the surroundings to our advantage.

I want you to get close. I want you to feel the truth. As you breathe in the air and as you live your daily life, drinking water and eating food from the earth, it is my hope that your outlook improves through learning the methods that have been time-tested through various philosophical concepts. It was compiled through rigorous study and continuous internal and external examination. All of which has been written in a way to allow you to focus on the importance of transcendence through logical understanding or greater passage into the known instead of existing in the world of the unknown that is our inherent way of life today for most of the population.

Throughout the ages, humans have had a primary focus on the written word as a main method of communication; based on these concepts, not only did they continue the process of writing, but they also improved upon it. Therefore, it is up to works like this book to present a peaceful and easy to comprehend view of the subjective human life from an individual perspective, in hopes of making your life easier and more productive. From that point of view, we could, in fact, agree that this is a self-help book and that my interests as an author are to help you lead an improved life, one that is fulfilling, by helping you recognize the truth of your internal self.

I would also add that the method of writing is slightly different, as some of the text is presented in a way that details the three primary concepts that are divided into five different sections which exist on the **Operational Juncture** that is your life or the turning point to a new beginning. This is beyond important, and it cannot be stressed enough the amount of power that a person can have over life when they finally realize where they belong in this world. Having a sense of belonging is essential to pure understanding and achieving a sense of control.

The point of this text in its entirety is to enhance the reader's experience by bringing them 'into' the story of who they are as individuals. This is achieved by bringing light to the symbolic methods and introducing the reader to a world that may have previously been unknown. For example, we start with three distinct points of reference that exist at any given point in time and are considered non-visual symbols. These create the five realities that exist in the symbolic mental world of human existence. We initially focus on the first chapter, "Time," which is about the ever-existing struggle that we have with persistent change and not so much the human concept of the clock with the seconds ticking away.

In the chapter "Origins," we cover the initial struggle a human must encounter at the beginning of their life and the destiny of an individual which is first established in their origin. "Origins" consists of the concepts such as Birth, Needs, Awareness, Society, in addition to other topics, all of which lead to a system of thought in its entirety. These elements are key to understanding the internal self and bring forward the three key ideas and the five realities that are offered within them as concepts that bring insight and consideration to what is called the "Three-Point Path of Change." This is another name for the three methods that are covered in the text—Theory, Action, and Change.

Therefore, the first of the three specific concepts is **Theory**, as it is common for any human to use rational thought when referring to any type of example which gives knowledge of or provokes transformation. This part of your life consists of "Life and Death," "Technology," and "Union." Next, after the human determines aptness for theory, he or she can excel to **Action**, which consists of a chapter on being a "Worker." This action is primary and is the way of our world as the actual movement comes from activities in work environments. This chapter on action or the worker is sometimes considered a fighter or warrior, and as it is a part of life that a clear majority of the population deals with on a regular basis, constantly striving for something so much better than themselves. This can be immensely difficult for people depending on their position in life.

This process is used in a human thought process contained in an **Octahedron**, which we know is a shape, but for our purposes in this text, it is a special symbolic system. Finally, after the human evolves in the process through gaining aptitude and defining a role, they reach actual **Change**. This is the final step where you merge with the universal mind that already exists in your psyche, which is the point of reaching a certain condition of accomplishment. The universal mind is the final reality as the book then attempts to normalize the entire work to a degree, making the reader aware of the truth of the mind and how important it is to look at the individual and constantly question the cosmic divide as it occurs in your perception.

The different realities that we focus on in this book are almost like levels of existence or stages of living, which is something we have to consider in order to endure and continue developing ideas from this perspective. These concepts are also subjective, but formulate some objective view of the world landscape in the way human interaction occurs and what we should expect. It is through "Origins" and other chapters of the book that I may briefly give practical examples of what has been said to help the reader make sense of the complexity of the system presented. The goal therefore in the simplest sense is to make this a 'handbook' for personal development and insight. It should act as a type of advisor that can help you finalize a viewpoint regarding a subject in your life that you may find confusing or be unsure about, to develop it into a positive experience for lifelong adjustment.

These ideas do go beyond the 'handbook' point of view in some respects, and this work could easily be misconstrued as a psychological, metaphysical, or religious text. However, our method is to go beyond this definition and into a realm of insight that does not currently exist for examination of the subjective self. The overall view exists from many thought processes, and beyond the works of general existentialism, epistemology, and metaphysics, and then focuses on introspection or self-awareness to benefit the human in complete comprehension. On a similar note, this book differs from an academic textbook because it is my personal perspective and designed to be a summary of subjectivity, for the purpose of leading to greater action.

It is, and always will be, an admission by myself to not neglect that as an author my personal point of view is not ignored for a great majority of the text. My experiences are used to create a baseline of thought as any good philosopher should initiate in the beginning. The goal is to go beyond this struggle to real change, to make a real difference in people's lives. To know this 'change' is to understand the way time works in our world, and how it is perceived. How we go from one second to the next, to live and die by the clock. Therefore, time is at the beginning of this text in chapter one because we want to know that without time we would not exist, but we are also at war with it. It is only through my experience of the external world that I would have been able to elaborate on these key concepts such as the chapter on "Life and Death," which is focused on the beginning, middle, and ending of the human life. While the extreme scientist might ignore a majority of the subjective views on human existence, it is up to the philosopher to focus on those more obscure references that make up living in this universe.

Unfortunately, like many other humans, I have been through a few major life struggles but would not claim to 'feel as you feel' or 'understand what it's like,' as people sometimes state in this description. We should examine certain points of view that led to a particular conclusion that may directly relate to the establishment of the systems involved. An example of these experiences comes from the "Technology" chapter.

The amount of work that went into creating the concepts contained in "Technology" was beyond the norm. You cannot even begin to describe the involvement with developing this key reality from my point of view. I sometimes feel that most of my life exists in this chapter, but it is obviously so much more than just my perspective which we focus on. However, it is through my experiences in technology there comes a specific point of view that others may not be familiar with.

The "Union" chapter focuses on those that we may have loved, still love, or will love in the future and is completely dedicated to the preservation of the 'dualism' in the symbolic system of the chain as mentioned in the chapter of "Life and Death." There is some visual context to this work because it is one of the few ways we have to break the divide that is the communication of words. In these images exists a serious attempt to portray what we will describe as a particular method but will be later detailed as fundamental to your internal self and the understanding therein.

Also realize that knowledge of this level can sometimes be lost to the tides of time and, depending upon the quantity of information, you will need to focus on these topics occasionally to prevent the disappearance of information through mental decline as you age.

The disclaimer that I would present is that no human knows everything, but we can all try to understand something to the best of our abilities, especially as we take part in the struggle that is our time on Earth. This book is not meant as counseling, nor can it replace actual medical care. Keep this book with you as a reference for your meditation and mental training, but you must always seek actual medical attention when needed. I do not have a medical degree and my expertise comes from a philosophical point of view. To give you fair warning, these are just words. What you do with these words is your prerogative.

While there are many texts that propose topics that relate to the psychological aspects of who you are as a person and what type of life you lead, this text focuses on the categories of experience and how you can look at your life from a big-picture point of view and analyze how important you really are, helping you determine what you can offer the world with the skills that you possess. These benefits focus on the self. When you understand your true nature, the world will open to many new possibilities.

This text is a compilation of the work of one human in his time here on Earth for helping others understand that which they may not always see at first glance. My experience may differ drastically from yours, but my time here may be shorter or longer than your time on the Earth; either way, I would hope that you use the knowledge contained in this text appropriately, so it enhances your own quality of life, as this is the complete intention.

You should also read other inspirational texts and formulate a well-rounded point of view regarding your own self-awareness, so when the time comes you may teach others of a new, well-constructed way of thinking from your own perspective. Someday, with technology, maybe we could transfer a lifetime of knowledge to one another, but until that day comes, it is in this instance that we would use this text as an attempt to transcend the normal method of communication.

There are so many reasons why this book can be used in your daily life to develop your key ideology, specifically to become so much more than you currently are. The key reason it is so important is because this is a story of you—the human.

Your story is the most important story of all, so it is essential that you recognize this in your daily life instead of falling into negativity or possibly even giving up and accepting failure or believing in defeat which happens to us all at one point or another. Instead, you must continue to be strong through the tough times and always persevere.

For this and many other reasons, this book is divided into specific sections as mentioned, each focusing on the importance of the internal and external mental world with the big picture being a story of the cosmological nature that is you.

Join me in the beginning of this amazing journey, with Chapter 1, "Time."

1

TIME

T ime, as we know it to be, is very obscure in its definition
but is ultimately the constant movement of any substance
that relies on an undetermined path to an unspecified point in space.
Time is, in fact, change occurring in our environment, and our way
of perceiving time originates from many different points of view.
When a change occurs in the real world, we find no way to reverse
the action or go back to an earlier point in our lives.

As an example of this, in common usage, we speak of
terminology such as past, present, and future when we think of time
as our way of communicating and measuring the actual change of a
particular source to its destination. In our minds, as a symbolic
reference, we imagine a one-way arrow from past to present with an
estimation of potential future events. From a scientific or rational
point of view, time is the fourth dimension and is a key subject in
physics as well as philosophy. This chapter is meant as a summary

1

or outline of the text that is to follow. If this book were a house, 'time' would be the foundation on which the house sits. In this sense, time is the essential ingredient for understanding the origin of who you are and understanding the desire to be somewhere else in life.

For the actual concept of time that a human is aware of or when we mention the study of physics, we are talking about a point of reference that exists in as a conceptual 'clock' which fulfills our daily schedules. The other, more philosophical, concept of time this text refers to is the actual change of substance (movement from point A to point B in the dimension) instead of the defined change in measurement (i.e. a clock on the wall). As humans, we use time to determine daily schedules and routines and, of course, for measurement. There is, in fact, a relationship between the clock-based concept and the 'movement of substance' point of view.

In this sense, we are focusing on the entirety of changes that take place at a given moment, so the connection between the two can be found by looking at a clock. If we ignore the idea that the clock moves for the purpose of giving us a number as representation, then we can see the hands of a clock as substance, moving continuously. The point we are making here is that this chapter focuses on the primary concept of time not as movement on a clock but actual 'change.' Secondary to this, communication is just as important because it allows knowledge transfer from the text in a book to the mind of the conscious individual, in addition to further involvement with the subjective mind and its movement through the language barrier. By subjective, I mean personal view of the world, not from the view of other humans, which would be objective. When you see the world from your own perspective that is considered subjective.

It is in this sense that both concepts directly relate to the idea of symbolism. When an object or idea is symbolic, it encompasses an idea or viewpoint that must be understood through inquiry. If you are unsure of a sign you see on the road, you would either look at a driver's manual or read about it on the Internet. That is just one example, but there are thousands of ways a human can relate to a symbol. The clock is symbolic of time but is not actually time itself, as the change and movement of the world and the universe are aspects of great complexity. So, from that example, we can see that the complicated nature of reality is reducible to a symbol.

Time is an ever-present container that is partially available to our view of reality, as it contains properties that are key to understanding the progression of the senses and where they form during a particular event. Memories, and even thought processes, are constantly shifting from one point to another. This is how time takes advantage of the human and forces a limited frame of reference from one observer to another. Look around you right now, and you will see a world that changes in an instant.

The environment around you will not be the same world you looked at a second ago. The colors will be a different shade because the light moved as well as many other objects. Not only are our memories from moments ago unclear of the world around us, but so is our vision as we see different colors in the same object from one instant to the next. Memories are not always clear and as they should be, but we may find that every instant in life is different, and every point in time has something new to offer us. It is through this information that we find ourselves in an event-driven reality which allows us to experience a world that only we know, from a perspective.

From birth to death, the war with time is being waged. Humans are constantly struggling to slow down the clock and attempt to control this force; but at the same time, we are at its mercy. The downside to this is that without the sands of time there would be no human mind, as it took a deterministic system to reach the point where we exist. In our lives, no matter what the action, we are all focused on achieving a primary goal or accomplishing a task in a specific amount of time, though at first glance it may not appear to be so. It is through the construction of a positive mindset that you typically find freedom from the complexities of life in this sense, and it does take time for the essence of knowledge that you retain to establish this sense of certainty.

It is only through the hourglass and the ticking of the clock that you will begin to understand the importance of the human lifespan and how there are many symbols in nature that give us insight into the purpose of the human experience which then leads to higher knowledge of the subjective self. You may find that as time slips away, you will have a greater appreciation for the present. There are symbolic standards related to this that we should all follow in attempting to understand these truths. In addition to this, we should work with each other as much as possible to follow the correct path.

All of the humans in your life present some kind of intelligence that relates to the information you seek. In this text, we orientate ourselves towards understanding personal identity and subject matter that is similar to metaphysics when we define the internal, external, and primary concepts of the self or the 'universal mind.' But for now, we should know that there are many points of reference, or parts, to not only your personality but also your existence throughout time. To define this further, we can say that these are separate ideas from the whole self, existing independently of each other but at the same time combining to create a type of order that one would find in nature as existence happens all around us, at all points in time.

Another important feature of time is human communication and the method of making connections. Without communication, we would not be able to speak to one another in a relevant manner that would assist either of us in achieving our objectives. At first, both concepts seem separate and unrelated, when we look at the path of time and chain of causality, communication, and decisions become interrelated. The idea of time goes hand-in-hand with communication, just as it does with change. While change is in fact time, decisions make a change, and free will is what a human being utilizes when making a decision that can impact the future decisions of another human through time and communication. It is in this subset of rules that we find technology being developed and created for the method of being assistance-oriented, forcing us to interact with each other in ways that can at times be invasive.

All that we do in life is based upon this concept of an action happening at point A and what happens as a consequence at point B, which is all a human really wants to know and wants to control— the future. To concentrate on what happens between these two actions requires that you focus on the past, prior to the initial action. While this can be complex, the concepts of both time and communication commonly provide you information that does so much more than reference your personal subjectivity as an individual. Through time we know that there are many decisions that you must make throughout your life, but there are even more paths that you can follow to reach a specific milestone as there is a multitude of events that take place in a chain of events.

The flaws of the communication method used by text is that the reader cannot understand with words alone and cannot bring amazingly-complex ideas into light because the language we speak is just a container of words, a simple method of communication and one of the oldest means of transitioning an idea from person-to-person with the intent of invoking a change. While it has withstood the test of time, the language barrier is still an issue in regard to information transmission throughout time. The same goes for numbers which are a representation of the quantities of objects in the physical world, at a similar point of view as text.

All of this must be combined with actual action which takes time to invoke a change in consciousness. Therefore, a book can only do so much to bring about special knowledge to the reader who must push themselves to achieve full comprehension of the text. This is intended to be a system of truth that goes beyond what I, as the writer, can put into a book for you to read. There is a multitude of ideas that have to be summarized and at the same time brings you to an awareness of the importance of time with regard to the observer.

To some, the concept of time traditionally exists as a known and understood system, which makes it a concrete base of knowledge that amounts to past, present, and future. To others, time does not exist, and all events fall along a present-only path where after an event happens it no longer exists. Along this train of thought, they believe that because the future has not happened yet, so it is not real. Probability is included in such a model, in addition to a number of quantum-level math problems that only a physicist would understand. Our focus is on the actual insight gained from the subjective method.

When examining time, we understand that there are those that believe that time is relative, which comes from Albert Einstein's theory of relativity. In such a world, each person has a different perspective of where they are and how much time they have at a given instant. This is indeed an interesting theory which has been the primary basis for so many books and lectures by scientists from all around the world. Let us, for a minute, examine a world without humans and think about what the nature of the universe could entail without the method, means, and insight that a human provides. If there were no people to perceive the world, then it could be argued that time would not exist. That is one of the first notions we want to obtain from our examination of time itself is that without humans time is not present.

So then, without time in the world, free will and the idea of determinism would not exist. In a world with humans, we have created this concept of time primarily because we have the urge to extend our power into any world where we are finite and limited. This is the importance of time and its existence: to give us free will, but at the same time, it attempts to force upon us a notable series of predictable events either of terrestrial or extraterrestrial origin. This is why we, as conscious beings, find it extremely difficult to tell the difference between something that has been predetermined to happen versus something that happened via our decisions.

We are inherently programmed by nature to believe without a doubt that decisions we make are forcing a change with multiple options as a result. Throughout history, humans have understood that a good portion of their actions are out of their immediate control. Due to this, we have enforced symbols in our lives, not only for communication but as a spiritual attempt at controlling our external environment, to go beyond the physical body.

The symbolism in our world is based on so many different viewpoints. By introspective mental practice, you will develop an understanding of theoretical principles that are essential to insight on advanced subjective. By subjective, I mean personal view of the world, not from the view of other humans, which would be objective. When you see the world from your own perspective that is considered subjective. Where you need to be in your life is entirely based on the decisions you make, and the consequences that result from your actions; this is where free will comes into play.

These choices are indeed finite and limited to your field of influence depending on where you are in life, but they are your choices and nobody else's, hence the 'free will' to choose. To develop as an individual, you will learn about failure on occasion, so it is essential to have a strategy when getting ready to battle the complexities of the external world so that you may prevail and be successful. It turns out that, over time, decisions are made that you have absolutely no control over. This is where free will comes to a halt and determinism steps in and pushes your decision aside and enforces the idea that our decisions sometimes do not have meaning.

Therefore, the decisions that take place in this world are, in fact, a basis for a chain of events that were determined prior to your existence. While we will talk more about this later in the text, the focus right now is on why the humans on Earth would be accepting to such control of their actions and behavior. The answer is that we would not; a human wants free will and the ability to control the surrounding physical environment as he or she sees fit, to be able to inflict their will upon an object. Without the ability to control our fate we would be living in an illusionary world. Obviously, none of us wants to feel like our decisions are not being taken into consideration. It is apparent that the human does, in fact, have the free will to make certain decisions that is why a good portion of the Earth as we know it has issues, due to the fact that flaws will always exist.

IN THE BEGINNING

The human who comes into existence in our era has much to learn about the world. For most of life, they go through the world unenlightened or by not being the rational human that could achieve so much more regarding self-understanding. For the world that currently exists, there are unfortunately very few people who can say that they understand the 'how' of our existence in their own words, from their own experiences. If this is the case, then the 'why' is even much more difficult to accept for those who may have some of the story but not all of it.

One of the main reasons for this is because of the straightforward, logical, scientific environment that neglects philosophical inquiry and creative thought. We will talk more about the symbolic environment that our minds exist in at a later point in this text. For now, we will focus on the seemingly paradoxical being that looks through our eyes to the world around us and uses the brain it's attached to in addition to the hands and everything else that the body allows for, but seems very limited beyond this – yes, we are talking about the consciousness. It is through its time on Earth that we find existence and the life we live on a daily basis.

The human mind forgets that the person standing next to them has the same life as they do. How this entire system works is not complicated, but accepting it is sometimes difficult. We must first define what it means to exist, to have a 'being,' to see through the eyes, and at what point consciousness or self-awareness is defined. Inherently, we know not to treat others as we would not want to be treated, and it is indeed relevant to assume that they could, in fact, have the same reaction as we would. On so many levels, it can be assumed that they live a life similar to ours and we should respect that connection.

We cannot forget what defines us as humans; we cannot ignore that in order to understand yourself you must know the truth of your existence and analyze yourself and the world around you, especially to determine what you want out of life. In our era, a human can do more with their life now than they could in all of time. Depending upon the culture or country a human is born into, they have so many opportunities to make their life better even with so many people competing for resources. However, to do this, the theory must be understood in the mind. What was once forgotten needs to be remembered for the goal of changing the world for the best. If not the entire world, then at least one personal, subjective world.

Time has allowed us to be here. At the same time, we struggle to find equality within it; it allows us to exist, as we have origins in the cosmos. We have to remember the one-to-many ideology, where at the beginning, prior to our existence, we came from one source, but now exist as many. It is essential that we understand our internal and external environment is constantly reverting to a 'connected' world as this source never wants to be separated entirely from each of its beings.

At the beginning of all that currently exists, before the idea of time and existence came into our view, we will describe this as the first point in time. This point will be defined as Point A, or the first event, best defined by the first letter of the English alphabet. It should also be noted that time did not exist before Point A, and that is exactly where the complexity arises because the universe was not yet in existence, and 'it' was timeless. The timeless void that we hear so much about in ancient texts existed before the universe, and then the universe itself was initiated by energy that we are not yet able to describe.

This goes beyond our rationale and questioning as it is the great beyond in human understanding, and attempts to determine who 'you' are subjectively. This is exactly why no theory that I give you will make complete and total sense, or fulfill your requirements. However, it was at Point A where non-time, non-existence, and nothing existed. It is entirely relevant to assume that time was initiated as a determined entity or energy which was forced by primary energy to expand and contract upon the void or, as we know them in science, 'energy forces.' In this case, the keyword is 'determined' because without the actions that preceded human development there would be no existence. The world is too organized and too precise to be completely random, and this is definitely something we want to believe.

At this point in our universe, humans with consciousness did not yet exist; and was too early for this kind of life. The Earth itself was not yet developed; the process took a great deal of time. Once again, that word 'time' is used, but there were no humans to recognize the concept of time. We have to ask ourselves if there was any delay in the time between the birth of the universe and the development of the Earth.

This is similar to when we go to sleep at night (neglecting the dream state); a human falls asleep and wakes up, the sun sets and rises in an instant. Another interesting point of this is that the expansion of the universe happened in a different period than we are used to. It is as if we perceive time differently than the universe follows its actions. An example of this is how at least a billion years must pass in order for anything interesting to happen. The earliest form of light happened early on, at least 10 billion years ago. The important fact to realize is that this idea is definable or knowable in a sense only through the eyes of our current existence – current time in our subjective reality.

However, once we get to the point where the formation process of the Earth starts, there is a strangeness that starts to appear. Science tells us that we are made from cosmic material and that our solar system existed at one point as practically nothing, but over time this changed, and as planets were created, so was the Earth. It started as just dust but ended in a formation. Understanding the Earth is key to realizing the importance of who you are as a person. The time that was spent in this life cycle was extraordinary, as we would obviously not see such change in a human lifetime. The element of 'existence' or life came from the perfect place at the perfect time scenario that the Earth has in our solar system or the areas of the solar system where planets can exist with life.

At this point, the organisms developed over time, but from **one source**. The key here is **one source**, multiple ends, but existing as the same source. Fast forward to today, and we see that whoever is active now is currently alive and connected to everybody else that is alive, and every other form of life on the planet. The origin came from one source, not multiple. Therefore, anything that is alive on this planet has just as much a right to live as you do, keep this in mind. Yes, you are alive—but this is your subjective point of view. So, as you read this, your personal point of view is different from that of another person. Or is it?

What if you are in fact that other person, however, at a different point in time? We can assume then that whoever is active at this point is the person who is currently taking action now. The **threshold**, which occurs when an action is repeated until change is forced to occur, is applied as well. Many actions in this world, and many decisions have a threshold where a 'breaking point' starts to exist and a decision that was once simple or impossibly complex is changed into something completely different. The further the Earth takes us with this existence, the more we change over time. The Earth itself is alive. This is present in many theories throughout ancient cultures. They believed that the Earth has a life to it, a collective consciousness. This is the essence of the universal mind, a special change in the deterministic chain of events that would normally dictate a path of rationality which is inherently connected.

We started out as animals; now, we are all a part of the same being, as the same consciousness event though we are separate in a sense. Imagine what the first humans thought, the humans that had the ability to utilize consciousness and the self-awareness. Did they recognize this ability in others? Alternatively, did they hunt each other down to take resources and start wars that could not be won? It can really be as simple as stating that we are all the same, as we all feel, think, and act the same under same circumstances, we are one the universal mind.

Each of us together is one driving force that works to achieve common goals like getting a team together to win an award, or for training purposes. No matter what the event, there will also be some kind of negative behavior that comes from the actions of the human, they don't have to be specifically stated. Even as children, we are told not to do something negative to another human if we would not want it done to ourselves. It is a truth to our existence that we have all forgotten and we no longer work as a cohesive unit to remember that we are made from the universe. We must never forget that the Earth was made from the universe. In our current era, we are unconsciously reconnecting ourselves to each other using technological means. This is due to the one-to-many concept, and the fact that the natural progression is to have one entity.

We fight these truths because we want individuality; over time our technological environment has forced us to be singular individuals as opposed to the driving force of the masses, but as it seems that over blocks of time this changes and fluctuates as the clock progresses. In the end, we all end up in the same place, so why not start at the beginning.

The question that you should be asking yourself is, "How am I me in this form right now, and not the other person? How I am the primary life, or the active one reading this book right now?" The person who is the active life is there because it is their purpose to connect with the physical world, primarily with the realities as specified in this text, in order to focus on one goal. Live the life and complete the task for that particular existence.

The active observer is the one who is living their life at this time. This concept starts with the issue of the secondary observer. How can they even be proven to exist when there is only one observer which is primary in the active life? You do not know with absolute certainty that other people exist as you do, but at the same time they are standing there in a human form. There are many ideas that provoke the thought that there is a threshold in the background of our lives that pushes us to perform activities that we are potentially determined to do as the primary observer, but that is time causing the change in our environment. Time is always there as the container forcing us to move in a specific direction but giving us the freedom to make the choices along a chain of events.

It is this change throughout time that allows an action to occur for the benefit of a human or their decisions. Free will comes from the human, and the decisions made on a daily basis. We have to ask ourselves, "What is the purpose of this life, and what should I do to change my life for the best?" It is important that you ask yourself these questions about your existence in order to completely grasp the drastic nature of our world, and the depth that you must go to actually make a change. You are never powerless in this sense; you will always be able to make a major change in the world because you are a part of the world, and the rest of society is connected to you even if it is not directly active at that point in time.

Sometimes other schools of thought lead to the idea that our long-term purpose on earth is to leave the planet and initiate the process of space travel. This is true to some extent. As an assistive technological force that drives our decisions, we find that leaving the planet is only the result of many centuries of trial and error. The inhabitants of the Earth need to move on to survive, and this might result in us utilizing technology to transcend the planet. We have to assume that this long-term outlook may not be as relevant as we think, considering at the current rate of overpopulation and negative changes we are making to the world (not just the environment but the social populace), that for this reason our species may not last another two hundred thousand years. The human race may die out. To get specific, the human race should be performing long-distance space travel in less than three thousand years due to current technology, and by two hundred thousand years we will have gone past the point of a 'space-society' and advanced beyond the current paradigm. The point is, do we really see this future from our current state of the world?

Think about a million years from now; where will humans be? As I have stated before, in time there will be certain people who follow these rules and understand the true nature and goals of our world and that we must find another way to continue our survival throughout time and space—but these people may be disregarded. As society destroys itself, certain people will move forward to assist. Depending upon their role in society, they will be looked to for inspiration and help during terrible times should they arise.

KNOWLEDGE AND HUMANITY

Being able to utilize the five senses is one part of the process, and learning is another that is entirely different. It's imperative that a human is able to remember and process memories first and foremost as this is a process of how the mind learns. Some people who are harsh in their words and negative in their minds would say that a human who cannot remember is less of a human. The idea is that if somebody is lacking the ability to recall memories they have in fact lost their humanity – and I tend to disagree with the real world practicality of this.

How quickly some people fall into judgment against those who may be unable to form new memories. We should understand that if a human has a mental disability that prevents them from obtaining new memories that they are not less than us, as when we look into their eyes we see a true member of our tribe, our humanity. No further justification should be needed in this case as we are merely providing an example of a philosophical inquiry. In a potential example, what if a person could not create new memories and was unable to deduce right from wrong or utilize their senses to learn new ways of thought? When thinking critically about this situation we might think that their personal identity has been lost and they now are less able to acquire knowledge. The point of this example is to determine if we are in fact our experiences? Do our memories make us who we are?

Having knowledge and the ability to remember the simplest tasks is essential because without it you would not be able to obtain what is required for your needs, nor would you be able to learn what is required to survive. However, in our era knowing a fact or a figure is a matter of typing some text into a computer. Also, for those that are less able to perform these tasks, our culture now possesses the ability of people who are willing to perform the service of helping others. The humans before our era did not have the ability to obtain information fast, as we currently do. They also did not have the ability to help others as those in our time. There is, in fact, a distinction to be made between information and knowledge. The former is the actual subject matter or data present, while the latter is how the human gathers this information.

This is where time and memories come into our search for personal identity, as it is through the cognitive nature of the human that we find actual change occurring throughout action and understanding. When knowledge is used and applied, it can be primary or secondary, known or unknown. Known information is essential to any given system, but when you reach the point of transcendence beyond the norm, such as in a spiritual sense or how a person might feel, in this sense knowledge itself is no longer an essential part of the system. Once you develop your experiences to the point where you have self-understanding, you can be assured that you are indeed fulfilling your role in our society.

If a computer program had the ability to think like a human, it would consist of information and therefore consider knowledge among its base abilities as we do for senses or life for that matter. To this machine, it would be considered natural. To know information is indeed essential to a given system, but this requires the ability to make memories. As we have stated, our memories can sometimes deceive us along with our vision and other senses. It is through this distinction that we, as a rule, cannot know everything, no matter how hard we try or what type of method we utilize. While knowledge does indeed spread among the masses throughout time through the senses, it is important that we dedicate ourselves to focusing on the mental perception of the world and knowledge of our limitations. You can focus on perception and at the same time be limited in your physical sensory abilities. As the essence and movement of time progresses, a change must occur where initiation to a knowledge-based topic forces information to shift from one person to another with a general path of beginning to end. The steps of this movement are in terms of usefulness. There is a primary usage that is mostly related to survival which leads to secondary activities which are typically 'desirables' or actions that we desire but do not necessarily need.

For example, say a new company creates an advanced technology that could help society with a particular task but keep it undisclosed from the public for trade secret or business purposes. Unfortunately, the consequence of not telling the public is hurting many people from a 'knowledge-based' perspective. This is where the gap of information is present. So, if knowledge is unknown to a general population at that point in time, there is indeed a gap in human perception of knowledge where one person may not know about something which could help others in the long run. This can apply to something that has recently been discovered where an inventor learns something new about a product but only a few people have any knowledge of this object or service. Obviously, in terms of business based ideology, this is common practice, but the point of our discussion is that there is a limitation present. It turns out that a great deal of time has passed for the information to spread throughout the society during this span of time. As time progresses, more people start to utilize the information, so the data is present but in the mind of the observers. Soon after this cycle of information goes through this process, it disappears completely as there is no permanent residence for the information on earth.

The idea itself may be present, and the data may be distinct in its presentation; however, the knowledge does not stay the same and does not remain in one place (in all environments including the mind). It is the act of creating a new idea that is essential to this process, as the idea had to be inspired from something like a series of actions. Is it possible that the new idea was inherent in the mind or was borrowed from multiple, secondary concepts, then utilized by the creativity of the observer to formulate an entirely new idea? Either way, with the changes of time, we find that the ideas vanish into the abyss. They are forever lost with the necessity that once necessitated the idea itself. It gives rise to the concept that there is a time and place for everything, especially from the human perspective, and that the knowledge we create has a complete ending and should be viewed as a temporary cause.

The knowledge that is shared with a society will depend upon its current level of competence and where it is in the long-term span of its civilization and technological expertise. Therefore, from an objective perspective, it is best to share knowledge as much as possible so that the information in question can be shared accordingly within its lifecycle. Communication using these methods through language is in fact, the only real way to transfer information from person to person, ultimately some sort of symbolic method. So, it is in this sense that we find all we know of the world is simply what exists as a temporary perspective at a point in time, and the communication we utilize is our best option in self-examination. What exists from our perspective is all we really have to ensure our continued improvement.

PRACTICAL APPLICATIONS

Since this book can get in-depth with topics related to the self and subjective inquiry, this section is included to summarize the work at the end of each chapter. This is so that you, the reader can make sense of the text that has been written and make sense of it in a way that the person reading the text can use directly. I would not want to write a book where the person reading it cannot immediately take some kind of control of their life.

To summarize what has been talked about, we see that over the span of millions of years the human race appeared out of the cosmos and now lives in its own internal system. Only through the movement of time does the human utilize communication. The abstract notions of a consciousness are even in existence because of the changes that time has initiated. For our personality, we develop an informal approach to this world and its constructs, always looking for a way to move forward in time.

The first topic that we can take from this is having some kind of **positive approach**, which would greatly enhance what is essential in your life, then learning how to approach **change in life** or **time management.** I realize that the two are completely different, but the point of the first part of the chapter is to let you know that your time is very limited; we all have a chance to really make a difference here on Earth, but before you can be helpful to others you have to be helpful to yourself.

In the chapter, "Worker," we will focus more on managing the time you have in your daily work life, because I can only assume that this is where you are starting from. If you are indeed coming from the beginning point where no work has taken place, then you would need to approach this differently. Your outlook on life would need to be adjusted to completely accept that when you look at another human being, you should be seeing yourself; be the person who looks at another with complete respect and understanding. Try to understand where the other person is coming from with their point of view and accept their opinions—even if they do not understand your own.

While it may seem irrelevant at first because this is a book about origins of the self and subjective realization that leads to change, starting with how you look at the world makes all the difference. If you are a negative person, you cannot make progress with any new ideas, as they would be beyond your rationale or willingness to some degree. This leads to another point, which is learning how to obtain the **will** to move forward. The strength of the internal mind can be found by accepting who and what you are: a fragile human on an Earth flying through space. You must accept that the universe is vast, and you are but a spec. Life matters, but it should be plainly accepted that your internal strength should be willing to take in these new ideas with great pride as your entire existence is absolutely a miracle.

Ultimately, this book does actually contain your **goal** in one way or another, as well as your achievement. This book also should guide you to the end result or what you hope to achieve due to your work. As stated before, the theory of your life is contained in a symbolic system that this text explains and also in the actions that you should take to fix, improve, and optimize the world around you.

Finally, the ultimate changes that have been made are only yours unless you share them with the world through direct communication or creations that resemble memories. It is through your will that you make the world know your true nature of who you are. True **free will** is utilized by the human through time and energy, and it is the one way we can accept that our decisions actually matter and are making a difference.

Therefore, we have determined that the 'will' is present, but sometimes this freedom to decide can only be acquired through hard work and determination, forcing through the negativity at parts in life. This book will speak more about the details of such activities. For example, when you wake up in the morning and follow your normal routine this can make you feel trapped—it is important that if you want to make a major change in your life then you must leave seemingly 'normal' portion of your life where you are comfortable. Doing this will allow you to start with small steps, leading to the larger goal of transcendence.

Actions and Thoughts:

- Recognize that time is change and it is the container that we exist in.

- Recognize that any person in the world could be you right now – and what that would mean for how you treat them. Without knowing exactly who they are as people, focus on what it would be like to be in their position.

- Understand what it means to be symbolic and how symbols are a method of communication either by direct or indirect means.

- Take a genuine interest in science and cosmology in order to understand the origins of the Earth.

- Know what it means to come from 'one source' in the universe.

- Recognize the 'thresholds' in your daily life.

- Question knowledge and information around you and know that true 'knowledge' may not be attainable.

- Begin the task of creating your own personal philosophy using the world around you as your framework.

- Begin to ask what it means to live a positive life.

- Start learning time management skills so that you utilize these ideas in peace. Sometimes, people who are busy lack the ability to take time out for themselves.

2

ORIGINS

B eyond the complexities of time, space, and reality, we can propose that everything in the universe has both a beginning and an end. There are many different types of beginnings and they can originate in the cosmos above us, in myths, or in stories about any point in time that a human can think of. Some of the most interesting origin stories come from the most complex systems. In this sense, the system of life on Earth is complex. It is amazing that the human race arose from a multitude of undefined and utterly chaotic movements over time.

For the purposes of this text, we are not following a specific type of religious point of view when we refer to 'origins' but rather a philosophical start of the human condition which was created from a specific type of event that occurs at the beginning of a story. We focus on the actions in between the beginning and the ending, just as it could, in fact, be argued that certain struggles are a part of daily life. This story also encompasses the lives that you interact with on a regular basis as part of the cycle of all change and movement at an original point in time.

Whether you use a symbolic narrative to describe your origin or you use a factual account, it is all human-created.

The concept of a beginning is time-based and relies on a method by which a point in space is referenced and de-referenced as an ending, all of this within a chain of events that is broken to introduce a new perspective when a new perspective is introduced. There is indeed a common theme of repetition throughout nature as it becomes ingrained in your mind. You are familiar with this theme because it is in fact what you consist of as a human because the cycle of daily life consists of this familiar chain of events. Every part of your being has these complete and common points of reference and this will sometimes have a personal impact; because perspectives that exist in this chain of events can cause unforeseen events both good and bad. If you live in a world where you constantly make the wrong decisions you are only causing yourself harm when you could utilize the chain for positive results.

From the highest order of perspectives comes the first and most important example of this instance, which is your own birth. It is your story, and it is of great importance, because it is in a realm of its own creation. It is a story that subjectively would include so many concepts and theories about your own life and internal formation

29

from an amazing first-person perspective. This is of an internal origin, sometimes confused with religious ideologies as there are many creation stories, and some of these stories have similarities in all of the key texts in the world on consistent origins. The beginning of a human life can be directly correlated with a religious creation myth because they offer some similarities, but more appropriately a human will associate symbolic notions with their life and the importance therein.

We should approach a method of looking at our internal and external self with the highest respect for those religious idealists who strive to make the human experience better from a subjective methodology. It is important that whatever symbolic method you ascribe to, that it does not cause negativity to others. In this sense, the philosophy of metaphysics will be mentioned as the end goal of the religious endeavor because its focus is independent of religion, and therefore focused on the actual substance that the world consists of externally. The ultimate goal is to focus on the self or the transference that occurs between internal and external. There are two ways of looking at this situation, one with you looking inward and the senses picking up the external world with the second being you looking outward with the senses picking up on the internal world. This behavior and perception from both points of view will allow you to adapt over time to develop new ways of thinking. This new action-oriented thought process is where the universal mind originated from; it is the real you.

It could then be said that when a person arrives at some

predetermined point in time based on their personal decisions, they have in their mind thoughts that were already existing at that particular time. These thoughts in question are composed of a material substance which makes the human form a mental incarnation of its universal constructs. It is, therefore, our goal to determine when the containment and activation of the personality appears in the mind of an individual to completely understand the view of that particular entity at that time frame. The human mind at that moment contains a process of thoughts whereby the movement had occurred at a previous point in time. This visual construct exists in the mind of the individual at that time, but only at that time. The visual memory is reproducible in the mind, but not its original entirety. Even a photographic image does not convey the true nature of the original situation.

As a human being in the world, you have an origin story and reasons for the specific actions along your path. There are various types of origins. The first is the mythical origin which takes place in the creative; however, the real world as an introduction to the first reality of your existence: the way in which you came to be a human, or how you were established. This mythical usage of the thought process is the kind of story that you tell others, and even yourself as it is the way that you want to be perceived. The story is essentially your beginning as memories will allow at that point in time. You know your own story very well, but where was it pieced together from and how did it come to be? It can be assumed that most people remember their past very well, but some do not. In this instance, people tend to create their own past based on actual truths. There is no intentional deception in this sense, only through the ignorance of the mind not being able to remember the entire story. Regardless of where the story comes from, we must look at the final product of the origin that you find yourself in.

This story of you, the one you tell yourself, is the most common origin story that sometimes becomes more important than your true external, objective story—which needs to come as close as possible to the external story that you tell others. But how can you develop a story internally if you lack the memories of those particular actions in the past? You have to learn more about your past from those that would remember you including friends and relatives. If you are hiding from your past, then this is a great opportunity to ask yourself what you are hiding from. This is the singular story of a human, but then there is the story of what is beyond the norm that can be something spiritual, a compilation of group creation myths such as those about masses of people in cultures that have performed historical acts. These types of stories are told by humans throughout the ages and is very common in religious organizations which to most is more than myth or a story; it is a way of life.

The self-developed origin story that we should be focused on is the story you tell of the life that you have lived and the actions you have taken thus far with as much truth as possible. There are points of reference that will assist you in understanding the primary theory which can be gleaned from this text, and then the steps you take will be entirely based on personal potential, resulting in changes that will take place in your life as a result of positive and fulfilling actions.

BIRTH

The complex life cycle of a human mind starts with the birth of the individual where all of the eyes of the family gaze upon the beginning of the life that has entered the new world. A human being is brought into the first stages of life where all the rules and philosophies of the world are now alive in the essence of the entire planet, especially when it comes to the thoughts in the mind and the beating of the heart. When a human is young, they are not accustomed to the environment they exist in quite yet and therefore are the responsibility of another human or group of humans. It is the parents that must take to heart the importance of this care that must take place throughout time. The beauty of the child should be exemplified through the eyes of the father and mother, who in a sense are the creators, and it is through the humans who care for the child come the most important of actions.

Their minds are racing to come to terms with the new life that has been bestowed upon them. They could not be happier in this moment as they hope and pray that this lasts forever. They have been given the opportunity to transfer their own knowledge onto a blank slate that they can indeed call their own, imparting their own experiences to a new generation in hopes of actually making major changes in the world. The mother and father are essential to the continued understanding of your personality and the decisions you make daily. As we look at the family environment and how it is defined, we find that to some extent, the masculine and the feminine aspects of the mind are established from the family to emphasize the origin of the individual from a biological point of view.

The internal 'self' begins learning the needs of the family early on through the parents, developing various methods to understand and

34

become aware of solutions to problems that relate to the group. Being a part of the family, this child has already become important even before he or she has met the rest of the elders in the group. Usually, those who encounter children have a need to assist because in the back of the mind there is a need to continue to help others. No matter what, at this point, it is now certain that this child is destined to be in a family. If it doesn't turn out that the family maintains, then a different path will form on the chain.

A family doesn't always continue on because people separate as time progresses, but we are concerned with this particular instant. We can be interested in the current moment, but it should be understood that there is definitely a truth that sooner or later the family will diminish to a smaller number of individuals. There are many expectations for the new human at this time, and he or she will struggle to live up to certain standards no matter how trivial they may seem. The human will be put in a position to gain power and respect, and even before the child can speak like the elders. The rules are there for the human to become skilled in the tones that make up the language of the culture.

For this child, the rules of life and existence cannot be understood yet because their method of understanding does not develop until later in life. Someday soon, the child will walk upright. In doing so, he or she will be defined by taking part in the society of men and women who have experiences in the world already and may be in competition at this point. As the human grows to adulthood, he or she will take their place in the chaotic work world and will strive to achieve order throughout the senses, using all available methods. The work to be completed at this level is massive and time sensitive, as key decisions will need to be made.

The human will ask so many questions such as, "Why didn't anybody teach me to do these things?" or "How could I do such a thing?" These will be repeated throughout the years. The parents will try so hard to respond with, "We did not know that things would be this way." The last statement is most likely true because they don't have all the answers. Regardless of the situation, there are only certain times when we will feel perfect with our lives, and these include holidays and special occasions when the group gathers to take part in celebrations in an attempt to forget about the problems in the world and to hope for the best.

The human desire and yearning to validate activities for the future and know the way it is 'supposed' to be will always be in the back of the mind. The mind wants more than anything to be accurate about the events that take place during a specific period of time and to build strong memories. We seek to enhance the rhetoric that the mind entails as there is an inherent desire to know an idea or how a particular action works because it's a 'need.' We throw this idea into a collection of concepts and ideas that, for the most part, are survived by scientific rigor and philosophical inquiry. All of these concepts fall back to the need to control not just our environment, but each other. When we need to know a topic sometimes our survival instincts are accelerated, and we revert to what we were like before adulthood.

The ideas of the universe, the world, and our consciousness are the key points to examine in our life. There is importance in these ideas, but more specifically how we can make the changes, how life can sometimes seem unfulfilling, but most of all how life cannot be underestimated. As humans, we are constantly trying to complete a need, or a desire, for something greater. A majority of the time this need is for food, water, or some other kind of essential item that we know from the basic survival instinct. Other times, there are the needs which fall into the sociological point of view, which is not always a rational point of view as it does not always agree with each and every person in society. It is on these occasions that life can be cruel to us by throwing us in a situation we did not expect. At the same time, we cannot lose our motivation. It is at this point you must pull your conscious mind in the right direction.

In this sense, one must conform to the rules present as it is in the best interest of both them and those around them. We live in a society where the baseline experience is forced to be lived in the beginning, and we have equalized the movement to create order where there was once chaos. There is a 'normality' to our daily existence as domesticated humans, as we all have a chance to experience life at the baseline. This is where the law comes into our chain, the law of the humans which focuses on giving equality to those of all ethnicities. It is that which humans have strived to provide each other through all of the pain and suffering of war, fighting against each other over incoherent desires. The human race has in this instant determined that it will be better to itself, wanting to some extent to follow suit with the possibility that we all exist as each other, at all points in time.

NEEDS

As mentioned, some of these are the 'needs of the people' because they fall into many different subcategories. Many times in

38

our life it would have been useful to have all the answers when making a serious life decision, or at least to know that the outcome would change the entire basis of a life experience. As we continue through our lives, we might find that a simple decision turns out to have major consequences when that was not what one intended. However, sometimes the experience loses its value when you have all the answers. Imagine if you knew it all. What would the world be like to you? The levels of existence can be compared to a tree where the branches expand as time progresses and the leaves accumulate like successes or failures throughout our days.

The tree is at constant movement along the path to the future and needs time to consume the water from the Earth, but also needs delicate external influences for continued advancement as it is constantly evolving, much like personal self-improvement. Because like the tree, the human life starts with birth when the mind is being overwhelmed by information in an over-stimulating way.

At this point in the life of a human, at the point in time that exists during the chain, the power to achieve goals is set forth by the symbolic notions that are predetermined by physical characteristics. Tall versus short, thick versus thin, the genetics of a human is inherent in the DNA of the human, as it represents the substance of life itself. As the tree of life and knowledge grows, the more branches are created and lived upon; where they end up is not always up to the human to decide. Even at this time, a life has needs. The interest in needs only strengthens in the human as the days move into the future.

Typically, the need for a deity is put aside in order to sustain food and water. It is true that divinity is a coping mechanism for the difficult nature of the society and the people in it. In ancient times when humans had needs, they learned to hunt and forage for food which led them to understand what it means to kill another animal out of hunger. Rarely was hunger put aside in these situations, as it was and continues to be a priority for most humans for their continued survival. During these times, if food wasn't available, or the crops were not plentiful then the humans would look to the deity for blame, and then potentially for guidance. The importance of this thought process is that when humans are faced with complete uncertainty, they look above to the heavens or beyond the norm for survival assistance.

The survival instinct is the act of sustaining life and maintaining stability when introduced to things that threaten the body and the mind in the physical world. The natural world can be beautiful, but it is not without its dangers. The primary needs are what a human must acquire when living in a dangerous environment, and this can both a physical and mental strain on the human. The needs that must be fulfilled include food, water, and shelter, but also it is essential to have clothing and protection from the dangers of the earth.

These concepts are defined as needs, but some can also be considered wants by human standards as we now live in an era of elegance and continue to be ever-present in a world where we have forgotten the methods of survival, and what it means to be hungry. It is then the goal of the self to determine what it means to be gratified by physical sustenance or by mental stability. We should know and understand the context by which we eat food, and drink water, but more importantly where it comes from and how much is actually on earth to sustain the population.

The personal identity of the self is not primary when it comes to the needs of the human. There should be clarification in this statement because, above all, people are working to find themselves. In this instance, where personal identity is concerned, people will put aside who they are to provide food and water to their family, but once this need is fulfilled there is indeed a great search for the internal self. The human mind has a picture of itself, the origin that it tells itself to fulfill a desire, goal, or way of thinking. We have to assume that in the modern era, these requirements for food and shelter are no longer primary mental needs for many of the current humans. It is not entirely understood by people who are no longer hungry because they have forgotten the truth of our world. Once hunger is satisfied the goals change to become more spiritual, and the mind tends to wander into areas that it would not normally. This is different in our time because we are no longer hungry.

We can indeed look at the simple acts in life by taking time out of the day, but the problem is that we let their emotions and potential wants get in the way of what is important, which is self-understanding. This in and of itself takes a great deal of time. For those who cannot schedule or manage properly, they will find stress and frustration prevalent. Previously, when men and women were 'wild,' people killed animals out of need. Human hunger can cause a person to be scared and force them into a position they may not want to be in, especially in the wilderness.

The first humans most likely did not give much thought to the animal they were killing, unless they had an emotional attachment to it. They were most likely starving, and they probably worked very hard to find various ways to fulfill their hunger, through trial and error. In our current era, it is common practice to kill a mass amount of animals to feed the populace, with the end result being that the person eating the food never went through the ritualistic process of killing the actual animal for food. We separate ourselves from this act; the same goes for funerals and the death of a family member because of the fear of death. Over time, the act of killing the animals for food becomes the norm, but we can assume that in the back of the mind of the individual there are issues present, but not yet on the outside depending on their personality.

There are two ways to look at the masses. First, you look at people and accept that each person is their own individual, has personal needs, and views the world from a subjective basis. Second, you look at the population as a whole has many of the same needs, and when leaders start down this path of objective incoherence or forcing themselves to be on the outside of a situation where they should be attempting to learn about the subjective mind of their audience, they are sometimes on a dark path which could neglect the few in favor of the many. The key is to limit the number of people in specific groups so that all humans can be related to appropriately, similar to a team-oriented environment. This is 'business thought,' as our world is evolving even through negative activities. Another issue with regard to this is the leadership required for each particular subset of people that are in a group environment.

They are all going to possess the same desire for a particular need; primarily this is the first needs—food, water, and shelter. Obviously, a human can only go so long without these resources, which is key to understanding the essence of this experience. A human starts out by being a 'planner' because they must constantly be preparing for the next available need, primarily for continued existence, or he or she will die.

The point we need to take from this is that a human will go to great lengths in order to sustain their needs; this is their survival instinct. Some of us have forgotten what it is like to be hungry; this depends on our society of origin.

SELF-AWARENESS

There is a major distinction that will be made in this book on some occasions regarding what it means to be a human and possess logic versus what it means for a machine to use logic and the conclusions one draws upon when it comes to developing a method of observation to essentially determine the truth of existence. The reason we cover this in origins is because we can see the beginning of machines that will someday be considered conscious. It is important that we start at the logical beginning: initiating a point of view regarding the consciousness of the machine. If we cannot understand ourselves, how can we possibly understand the machine that we have designed, and what happens if it starts to recognize our faults?

It is in the mind of the rational object, whether man or machine, where we find the most important part of the origins and the comparison of which seems relevant to our analysis. The technical details and decision-making process of the machine are obviously much different from that of a human, and in some ways very simple. Clearing the mind of raw data for the robot is, for the human, 'replacing' thoughts with other ideas or entirely forgetting about them. The difference in this is that there are many other ways to simplify the thought process. For humans, we can see and hear our thoughts or our internal voice. But does a machine have this ability if we do not program it?

We may wonder what the life or essence of the robot would

consist of in this sense: if we stood there and agreed that "yes, it appears to be alive," then what can we say about human nature and ourselves? There may come a time when human nature may be obsolete. We will wonder how it all happened, that the machines had learned so much over time. Just like the tree of life, a machine would also have to make decisions similar to humans as there are many branches in the chain of events. We have to wonder if those decisions on the chain would be as difficult for the machine as they are for the human. Based on actions and consequences for given situations, the continued development of new perspectives found in the human psyche shape and mold us into viable members of society, and these same activities can also break us down to what feels like less than nothing. A machine would not 'feel' the importance of the decisions, but quantify the outcomes into numerical objects.

The journey of the self with a community of people is not always set in stone. The ways of the masses seem unshakeable in their glory and judgment, but they are changeable based on the given stimulus such as those found in advertising and marketing. The changes and needs of the human are realized in our elders, friends, and extended family, from where we find a world of personal experience shattering the norms that we greatly assume are correct about our daily lives. The constant view of the subjective mind is about learning and developing a greater understanding of the most important aspects of love, union, joy, and so many other positive elements or 'categorical essentials,' which we will cover shortly. Through personal experiences, we must learn lessons of success and failure which give us good or bad feelings. It is only through education that we can learn the values needed to understand the constructs of law and ethics, and therefore cultivate the lowest levels of chaos to our favor so that our goals are completely relevant. This level includes small changes that can lead to medium developmental results. An example of this is smaller decisions, attempting to do something simple for somebody that doesn't force a major outcome. In the long-term chaos at higher levels, we see massive changes to the populace, such as decisions that are made by a governmental body.

A direct effect of your origin may be to find a religion or belief system that caters to your being, heart, and mind. Speak the truth to yourself, and understand that nothing is permanent, as you may have originally expected. It is not necessarily a requirement to have a religion, but it should be a journey of truth from your own perspective. It should, however, be your goal to strive to understand yourself as best as possible and look at each day as if it were the last. In this sense, it is possible to focus on the past memories that we keep to ourselves, always knowing that we have them until a later point in time where age sometimes forces us to forget. It's best to hold onto the memories as long as possible, giving yourself the internal story.

To develop yourself in this sense will give you pride and enthusiasm to continue being creative and work towards life success. These are the ways of being human, knowing the finite and the divisible, the minuscule, and the fragile nature of the world. Once you know what it means to be delicate, you can completely comprehend what it means to be permanent. As with any other comparable language construct, you should know one extreme versus the other, as it provides a great experience.

For true origins to be understood we need to look at the base individual, the core of yourself, which exists in all you have ever known. It is not from this Earth, and not alien in the fictional sense of the word, but rather a universal truth that you must learn to understand. All problems, at a specific time, can be resolved by some method, and you need to believe in your mental capacity for understanding a given situation.

These origins will also lead us to **framing** which is a way to take a period of time, examine it, and act on a solution. Time needs to be looked at as a sense like sight or hearing and must be taken seriously as it is so precious. Daily life becomes a habit, or routine, which needs to be acted upon occasionally for the big decisions. The question posed is, when do we act on a habit? If this habit is good, then we should not always change the behavior. The random actions of the world sometimes change it for us when we are unwilling or unable to take the initiative. It is always so much easier to keep your life the way it is, no matter how unbearable. There are many people in the world that would rather suffer and then dwell in the depths of the unknown for a chance at success. The goal of this activity should be to take a 'frame' of an instant your day, where you actually stop what you are doing at that instant and consider the actions that you are taking, and think about the reasons.

To the human who is stuck in the daily routine of life, they may not imagine these concepts of origins to connect directly to other species of animals, but we will point out that animals do carry the 'being,' or essence of internal or external origin that defines the specific change at that time. As for living on Earth, the human has some basic needs to fulfill, and they are no longer as difficult to achieve as they were centuries ago; this includes the needs of air, shelter, water, and food.

While achieving the perfect version of these needs is not always that simple, your physical and mental well-being depends upon these needs being met even in the simplest form. For our current era, there are many people who have little knowledge of these needs and what is required to survive, as some people are caught in the wilderness and are completely unaware of steps to find food and shelter.

To be satisfied, the needs of the human must sometimes encounter such threats. This is another point where we see the rules of 'give and take' or 'push and pull,' and the methods that force a human to fight for something that they need for continued existence. It is through the logic of movement and the order that is needed to define this process, where order and chaos become symbolic and somewhat visual in the mind of the observer.

There are various threats that exist in the world, mostly those of the external environment beyond what one would consider 'home.' These threats emerge from security and fear among the general population, and are usually physical and mental. People in the world are not always nice, but some have the capacity for caring. There are others that will take the shirt off your back and leave you dead in a ditch if given the opportunity. Unfortunately, this is sometimes the way of the human, but our goal is not to be the negative person in this situation. There are all kinds of humans in the world, and some follow an ethical code while others do not. This is about how you want to live as a person, and the example you want to set.

The goal of your personality should be to do well and help others find their path in life. The rational humans must also learn to protect themselves; this includes having a method of self-defense. When humans are faced with threats such as these, most turn to develop friendships, which occurs when the singular human cannot resolve the situation. Another reason for this friendship is to assist with well-being, preventing boredom, and work on a monetary or trading system that you can use to obtain other basic needs.

This is not to sound superficial by any means, as the solution to these potential threats is to develop friendships which allows for a common language, security, and assistance in curbing the fear that comes with physical and mental threats. When you have the understanding that other people will want to harm you, this stance does in fact help you develop your defensive position. Through this grouping, social networks form in addition to trading and financial means. To most, these discoveries become realities in the cycle of life; however, someday your time on Earth will be complete. Unfortunately, we do not really have a handle on what is next. The answer to such an internal discovery I cannot give you, and you will in fact find your own answers during the personal journey. For now, consider this life the only chance you have to fulfill your purpose and reach your destiny.

The anxiety that takes place once a person realizes this truth is particularly strong because all that you know and understand could possibly go away, including all your goals and dreams of becoming something you have not yet become, among many other terrible mental constructs which we may not be able to accept yet. We would like to think this would not happen, so that is why we must make the discovery.

Most people feel as if they will live forever, and even a few never come to the understanding that someday they are going to die. This is a great internal discovery no matter how morbid it may seem, and a person who understands that tomorrow may be their last day on Earth will soon do everything they can to live life to the fullest, cherishing each minute as if it were the last. This is not some kind of great secret or hidden topic but is a major component to self-discovery. This doesn't normally happen to those around us, until the day they find out there is some kind of terminal illness and the doctor tells them that they only have a certain amount of time left on this Earth. If you have not had this actually occur, then you will most likely not follow through with the idea that you should live each day as if it were your last, and I'm only asking that you look at the perspective and see the importance of time in this sense.

The fact that the mindset of the fear of death occurs at all is important because when we look at the general population and ask the hard questions, such as, "Why do people act the way they do?" and, "Why are some people so extreme when it comes to religion?" It is possible that a reason could be that they were raised to look at death a certain way, and it stayed with them over the years, sitting in the back of their mind pushing them towards one decision or the other, always as an unknown instigator either for positive or negative reasons.

THE THREE POINT PATH OF CHANGE (TPPC)

Every realization is a **Primary Concept,** or mental reality, because once you experience the feeling of knowing a certain point of view there is very little that can be done to reset the knowledge in your brain back to what it was like before you experienced the process. I realize that many others before me have categorized the human experience into countless categories and terminology, but in this case, my goal is to simplify the entire spectrum of the human life, which is easily noticeable.

Some of the key **categories of truth** that directly relate to the primary concepts are:

- Birth
- Life
- Father
- Mother
- Family
- Death
- Desire
- Water
- Nutrition
- Health
- Shelter
- Security
- War
- Society
- Warrior
- Law
- Sex
- Union
- Leaders
- Language
- Followers
- Friendship
- Technology
- Love

- Patience
- Dreams
- Joy
- Comedy
- Senses
- Evil
- Fear
- Addiction
- Misplacement
- Suffering
- Sadness
- Ego
- Confusion
- Hope
- Boredom
- Home
- Communication
- Language
- Deduction
- Generosity
- Memories
- Religion
- Astronomy
- Observation

- Identification
- Aesthetics/Creativity
- Knowledge/Learning
- Philosophy
- Fate
- Hope
- Creativity
- Order and Chaos
- Numbers
- Logic
- Excess/Deficiency
- Sound
- Divinity
- Infinity
- Nothing
- Elements
- Time
- New and Old
- Color
- Light/Darkness
- Layers
- Shapes
- Direction
- Growth

- Attraction
- Movement
- Connection
- Free Will
- Determinism
- Race
- Subjective Mind

While these are important concepts or key elements that exist in the human experience, we should keep in mind that there is so much more that make up our daily life. There are many experiences that are not easily recognized and are harder for the human mind to immediately take part in without some kind of trigger object or actual everyday experience. For our purposes, this is all just words. The world of humans can be experienced in so many different ways.

The purpose of this is to look at the following path as a container for life experience and then develop yourself in practical ways from here on out. Ultimately, these have a purpose for survival in the external world.

The First Path: *The Path of Theory* is the way you must go when you want to end up actually taking action and making a change. Just as in any kind of religion or meditation, you must take part in the theoretical or knowledge-based system to learn how to perform a task. This is the first step to enhancing your life. Without theory, there can be no change. While there is a great deal of knowledge in the real world, we can only focus on certain topics which will have the greatest outcome of change in a positive manner. Change itself is the ideal outcome in any given situation. This is where you build your foundation, and it happens at all parts of life. You are constantly building theory in your life by being who you are, and existing on the Earth.

- **Life and Death**: The first reality is to understand that the daily life experience may not always be the most pleasant place to live, but it is all we have at that moment. This includes various aspects that define your self-awareness, life, freedom, and continued existence. In life, there is the big picture, there is the detail, but then there is what is beyond the big picture.

- **Technology**: The second reality is your modern world and the technological era in which you were born into, and how technology will continue to progress from the point in time you started to exist. It is important that you maintain knowledge of this. Knowing and understanding how technology evolves is essential to the continued development of your purpose in life. While you do not always have to take part, it is important that you not fall behind of where the general population is on the scale of technological advancement. This allows you to think outside the box, but at the same time understand others' points of view.

- **Union**: The third reality is to understand love and affection, or the connection that is involved when two people connect. There is a union where barriers once existed when two people who don't know each other become close to the point where a major connection is created. The focus in this section is also on society and building your own social group, including your family. To build your own social group as a male or female, you may decide to have children, and in this sense, union is one of the most important parts of your life.

The Second Path: *The Path of Action* is the dynamics of motion that results from the knowledge that you acquired from theory. Action itself has multiple frames of reference or ways that it can go depending upon the original path it was on in the first place. It is very physical, but can also be mental. In this case, the focus is on the actions in life that are sometimes monotonous, but essential to making change happen in your life. All of this is symbolic and takes some kind of relevant form to enhance your quality of living.

- **Worker**: The fourth reality is being the professional, or the employed, working to attain currency so that you can take part in the society of humans and ultimately use it to achieve your goals. Fortunately – or unfortunately – working in the modern world does not consist of hunting and gathering; it is all about image and how others perceive you. In some ways, it has nothing to do with skills or what you can bring to the table, especially in the wrong environment. It turns out that this all depends on the situation, where we would talk about having a work life and a personal life.

The Third and Final Path: *The Path of Change* is the last element in the universal substance of the mind. The change occurs at all instances when the theory is complete and actions take place. It is essential that the human understands that this is not just a simple action related from a theoretical point of view. The state of change is one that exists in time and space over a finite amount of time. From the human perspective, we utilize it in this manner.

- **The Universal Mind**: The fifth and final reality is being the thinker, as you must become the personification of philosophy and knowledge. To become an important part of the grouping, which will follow in this text, you must be able to think and rationalize beyond the basic survival mechanisms and learn creative methods in a given situation. The human needs to recognize that there is some advanced basis for reality and the chaos that ensues. Your mind will indeed save your life, and in all of the years that you exist on the planet Earth, there will be many instances where intelligence is tested.

Look now at your hand, and you will see the symbol of the five realities. I will not waste the paper, or your time, in giving you a picture of a hand, but that is the symbol. Look at your hand very carefully, and think to yourself, why five? Why not six or seven? Obviously, the test of time caused us to have five fingers on each hand, and not four or six; either way, this is who you are, and this is a number of objects. For us, the hand will be a constant reminder that you are in fact human and that you have limitations.

When we go beyond the five realities, a belief system starts to emerge. This comes from the balance that you find in the Earth experiences and how you, the individual, form the basis of comfort and understanding from the mother, the father, the environment, or from other personalities/participants.

The personal opinion regarding a higher power is essential to the construction of the life that is to be lived and what actions will take part when inside the system. There are those who choose to ignore this construct and neglect it entirely, but they can only ignore logic so long as it is essential to their continued development.

This is not to imply that you must believe in a god, but it is important that you look above and see the world around you, and recognize that there is an energy or 'container' beyond yourself. If need be, you can then enter into the belief of a higher power or the religious substance that is divinity, infinity, or nothingness, alternatively the belief in one god, many gods, or no god. Either way, a person believes in a substance. Even in nothingness, the 'substance' of life emerges. I can understand the meaning coming from these feelings; it is the direction of time which assists you in developing your personal meaning of life.

The development of an internal subjective meaning to your life is a combination of the "Path of Change" mentioned above and ultimately how you cope with existence and the questions posed to you. You must go past the irrational feeling of invincibility and know that your universe as a human is entirely limited, in order to live your day to the fullest and perform activities that go well beyond your comfort zone to enjoy life to the fullest.

Whatever your decision-making process is, you should focus on the factors of time and communication. It is essential to understand and remember that you are human. This goes beyond the obvious response as we are all a part of something so much greater than we are. The remainder of the text attempts to define the five realities of understanding by dividing the ideas into points of change.

PRACTICAL APPLICATIONS

When attempting to create a new method of internal analysis, one must sometimes accept that changing the way we perform daily activities is not always easy. A person must go beyond the norm of society and, in doing so, accept that failure could be present. If you are not ready to do so, then a hard lesson will be learned. The consequences of the wrong actions usually encourage new behavior at some kind of cost. As new information is acquired, the learning experience can then later be used to transcend the limitations of normal thought, allowing one to see results more clearly. This is where life **purpose** comes into question, and what you are really supposed to be doing in your life. Having a purpose in life leads to **happiness,** which is the point of this text. Ultimately, we all want to be happy. To find purpose, you must ask the hard questions and work hard to see the bigger picture. Always follow the personal path of change which can stem from hard work and determination.

Once you find your purpose, petty obstacles and issues that

would seem so relevant can be put aside, and you will able to look towards the future of life, to a new and brighter future. After the purpose is found you can make more relevant decisions, resulting in more appropriate life changes. Putting aside the negative feeling of hopelessness can be invigorating, and allows oneself to find motivation in a mindset that was once void of any positive, forward-thinking methods.

Actions and Thoughts:

- Find a purpose in your life, even if it is something simple. Look for an action that causes a positive feeling inside, but make sure that this action can be reproduced and is not hazardous to you in any way.

- Start to follow the path to learning what it means to be happy, and finding out specifically what makes you happy as a person.

- Know where you originate from and understand your beginning. This could be learning about your ancestors, where they were from, and how they lived their lives.

- Learn about the people from the past, before the modern era which somewhat falls into the ancestry area, but those who were not in your direct family line should be studied as well.

- Recognize your survival needs and attempt to minimize the items that you are dependent on, this could include certain types of foods that could be causing harm.

- Practice instances of "framing" in your life and what it includes.

- Learn the "categories of truth" and what they mean, even if they are your own meaning, and how they feel about you as a person.

3

BIRTH, LIFE, AND DEATH

T he first reality is very simple to initially understand, but it is sometimes difficult to conceptualize in a practical manner. Realizing the nature of life and death may take an undefinable amount of time. This understanding can take place after days, a month, or even years. The major concept to grasp is that life is not easy and some pain must be encountered no matter what your status is in society, and after a long and arduous struggle, you will leave this world, hopefully in old age after a path full of many changes and many different circumstances. You may not always experience suffering, and your life may not be stressful, but no matter the situation life will be experienced.

A few number of humans do not always make it to old age, but this is the way of Earth. The actions you take can make or break your life, specifically at the beginning. As far as you are concerned at this point in time, life is all you have. It is all that exists from the subjective experience.

The point in time you now live in is a result of past actions that are ethically considered both good and bad. Someday, you will have to take into account that your life will end, hopefully, in a positive place. However, during your time on Earth, there will be many different experiences. It is up to you to make the right decisions and form perceptions that are not negative, constantly trying to live in a positive world.

Your life is important to those around you, as helping those in need can become a major element in the chain of events that continue into generations to come. Therefore, the development of a method that includes internal and external understanding during your time in this reality is entirely relevant. If you knew your time was limited, would you make decisions more appropriately or with more drive and act differently? Would you push through the fear and negativity to a more positive solution, if you knew how important it really was?

The importance of any decision is underestimated by many humans due to the way society views our measurement of time. It is important from a deep and thought-provoking perspective to accept and try to comprehend that our choices have consequences that go beyond our era, and into future generations for lives to come including our children and grandchildren. Even if you have no children, your decisions still affect others in the future.

Imagine from your perspective how different your life would be if a person prior to your existence had acted differently in the chain of events. *Would* your life be different? It is possible that their decisions actually created your life; In that case, maybe the correct decision has been completed for that instance. It is about the tides of time, responsibility, and proposing the right answer to the proper question.

There are many choices and questions in life, and experiences that never become a reality because as humans we are afraid of the unknown and of what is beyond the door that lies closed in front of us. **Opening a door to a new experience can be difficult, but if you have never experienced the action of physically taking your hand to the door and pushing it open, then you will not know what is beyond.** You should try to adjust properly to the major decisions that life has to offer as they happen on a regular basis. Remember that the decisions you make are not always bad, and it is important that you do not assume that the fundamentals of life cause inherent negativity because a majority of the same choices that we encounter are completely out of your control and far beyond the scope of what we can attempt to comprehend as a human. This includes a potential action that was initially caused by an event probably before you were born.

The concepts of predetermination and free will definitely come into the subject matter when we talk about actions. You may start to question the possibility that even your most important choices, made on a regular basis, do not seem to matter much in the grand scheme of the universe. It's the daily life experiences that can be rough and sometimes cause the world to be unpleasant, but it's all we have and it's who we are, as a great majority of this is because of the system that we have unintentionally designed out of society. Self-awareness in your life and freedom to continue existing are specific points that we want to cover in this section. You exist solely in your mind and body, always trapped in the moment that allows you to relate to an action, never free of the connection you have in the seemingly one-track plane of existence that you are on at this point in time.

Sometimes it feels like this human form is all we know, and knowing anything other than our life does not even seem possible. However, it is the feeling you get when you say to yourself, "What else would I be?" The human is who you are, and that is what you should strive to understand. The importance of this cannot be underestimated because there has to be some other form of life that you could have existed as when you think about what is beyond. Otherwise, how could you exist differently as some other kind of being or entity? Your vision of being something else is a point that should be examined in a way that is visual and constructive. In a hypothetical situation, you could look at yourself and think about how you are human and not a cat or a dog, or even an insect.

When a person is tired of being themselves, sometimes they go through a phase of self-examination where they consider the fact that the existence they feel is sometimes exhausting and they may be disoriented to some extent, or possibly even malnourished in both the mind and body. It really does depend on the situation, and of course, there are occasions when you may need assistance from others. As it turns out, each person that is encountered on the journey of life will help you determine the outcome of your perspective. There are finite, but seemingly infinite, amounts of events that can occur in your life decisions which might make you feel negative in a certain way, but it is good to look at the side of life that appears infinite.

In time, you will most likely grow tired of the major decisions you will have to make as the years progress. The sounds, smells, and tastes will become repetitious, but you must find purpose in this disorder. That is the purpose of the self-examination, and where you must take your path, to a place of order. Yes, the world may grow monotonous, but it's important that you look at the entire system and find a positive path to follow, this way disorder becomes order. There is order in chaos, and you should find comfort in knowing that even the smallest decision in your life will turn into something major, and you can only hope it will be a positive outcome. In life, we have various coping mechanisms which allow us to deal with stressful situations, or emotions that we may find unpleasant. The ultimate survival mechanism is learning to deal with the changes that come about on a daily basis, as you constantly struggle with forcing time to be on your side. Remember, you are a human; what else could you possibly be?

The question you could ask yourself is, "Where did I exist before birth, and why was I born now as opposed to any other point in time?" These are just a few of the most important questions you can ask yourself, and it is important that you go beyond the norm in this inquiry. Looking to the external environment and questioning your entire reality is important and should be done as if your life depended on it. This can be performed in a positive manner, as you must look at the changes taking place in your life. It is in this inquiry that we need to focus on the baseline experience that you currently have in your life, beyond the chain of events that so judiciously takes place without your intervention.

It is right now that you can look around at your life and ask yourself, "What can I actually change?" You will find that there is a great deal of control you actually do have. Look at the chain of events around you and attempt to find a start to your journey, and ultimately imagine a great finish. Look to the future and estimate where these actions will lead, understanding along this journey that not all of us can know the future and the exact actions that will take place. Fortunately for us all, we can picture in our minds a great outcome to take part in the circumstances. This way of taking part in general events are not always relevant as humans don't have control over all actions in the chain of reality.

The path of life and death can be visualized in a manner that is not entirely difficult to understand or relate to and is completely relevant to the fundamentals of the life experience.

JOURNEY OF THE SENSES

Everything in the world has some kind of visual or auditory properties or is communicated through one of the senses, some kind of tool that would provide information to the viewer. In the case of this book, the visual aid or the text is two-dimensional. The purpose of the object then is so that you may use your previously-learned language to read the words, or view the image and interpret as the text provides. It is essential in our case that we understand that this in itself is a limitation of human potential.

We are stuck in a world where language exists in a specific dimension which can go no further than what our perception allows for that point in time. For example, we can use our sense of sight to determine three-dimensional objects. Without getting too technical or mathematical, we should understand that this is a 'representation.' The way your mind sees an object in the real world is based on your understanding of that particular world.

These points are all dimensions, and at the surface of the human interactive experience, there are four dimensions: height, width, and depth, or for our example X, Y, Z, and T for time. This is the normal method for representing points via general mathematics. It can all be very limited in a sense that when you see an object you are viewing its color and texture, but you can only form theories about where it was at a previous point in time, and also where it will be in the future, thus your time perspective. The purpose of mentioning this is because we will use geometric shapes in an attempt to clarify the true reality.

What you do not see in your world exists right in front of you, and is based on your perspective. The levels of how you perceive the world will indicate how you experience and remember what happens around you. It's about looking outside of the box you exist in, and recognizing that there is indeed a shaped and reducible existence or the 'box' environment. Humans have gone as far as to completely remove land so they can create shapes to live in, and that is only a small part of the psychology of the visual representation. If you look around at this point, you will see all items that were manufactured, were done so in the usual shape, and if not box-like then it's most likely near circular.

To understand the visual representation, we will explain further by giving a view of the objective qualities, but at the same time providing sensory cues that you may have experienced in your daily life at one time or another. In this way, the following information may provide you a 'model' or a 'map' of the universal mind and its lifecycle throughout time and space. Not all of your questions may be answered through this process, but it can be a beginning for your journey into the unknown as you follow the path of theory. The world around you exists as it would for any other person, with the exception that you, as the primary observer, are the one who is actively seeing the object in question. You do not exist as two people simultaneously, so the world you see is your own perception.

It is important that you first recognize that you are yourself and nobody else. Then the questions will start to pour in, such as, "How am I me and not somebody else? Why was I me at this point in time?" All very relevant questions when we refer to this type of philosophical mindset.

THE OCTAHEDRON

The Octahedron is a geometrical representation of an entire thought system, and its mathematical definition is that it is a polyhedron, which is a solid that exists in three dimensions as a pyramid does. Eight triangles make up the octahedron. This is just one of the shapes that some in a religious or occult context would consider 'sacred geometry,' but is also one of the 'platonic solids,' which is one of five shapes to be a specific criteria.

For our purposes, we will focus on the philosophical and visual representation that this amazing shape has to offer. This shape also appears in nature in many different ways, but the most notable is the diamond which is one of the strongest gemstones in the world.

Regardless of where it appears in the natural world, one can agree that there is a certain beauty to mathematical shapes and some kind of pleasure that a person gains from viewing these shapes, which is not limited to visual perspective. However, as we move further into the abstract methods, and the philosophical inquiry that helps shape your world, we must understand that this is, in fact, a shape itself, which is composed of lines, points, and space. All of these parts have specific purposes that force increasingly complex but fundamental understanding of the world around us. Using the visual senses, we can understand and know that this reality is true, and we unknowingly utilize this geometrical substance. While it is indeed symbolic in nature, and it is even spiritual to some. It is not 'real' in the human sense of the word, but beyond the visual and sensory dimensions; we seek to adapt to this mindset and further understand the path of the theory.

To break it down right from the beginning and simplify what I am about to make slightly complicated: We are living in the octahedron, but note that you do not physically see yourself living in the shape. It's all symbolic and exists as a mental projection. Before we continue into the intricacies of how this system works, there should be some kind of explanation. Therefore, from this point forward we will refer to the octahedron as the internal barrier.

That is, in fact, what the shape makes up: a seemingly infinite barrier that exists from point to point on the exterior of the substance, which means that in the interior, the middle 'empty' space between the lines and points is, in fact, transparent. Any object that would happen to pass through this would not stop, as the barrier is indeed transparent. The internal system of the octahedron does not pass this barrier of empty space because it is the reality inside the object. The reality and movement inside the octahedron forces the object to have its shape in the first place, as there is substance to the construct.

The limited point of view of one particular entity exists inside this system. This is just one path, and in the beginning of this definition, we choose to explain multiple paths which lead to multiple octahedrons. After this, the system starts to appear very different, but once one learns of the internals of the objects in question, there is a significant change in understanding and coherence. See the picture below to see a basic octahedron and its shape. In this picture, we have the lines, points, and empty space.

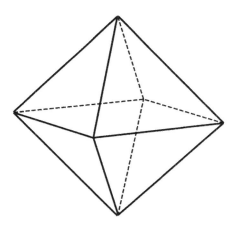

The Octahedron consists of 8 faces, 12 edges, and 6 vertices. It is a Platonic solid, which consists of eight specific equilateral triangles. For our purposes, we view this as the symbol of the current plane of human existence from the subjective observer, at one chain of time or 'grouping' that has an operational juncture or a 'current' place in time. It is important that we understand the contents of this structure and its external environment.

It is hard to imagine such an object that would encompass all events, as it would be enormous. However, we should ask about how large is it when compared to the universe? Obviously, when you walk or look from right to left, there is a recognizable way to determine that this is, in fact, the shape we exist in, but it is just a symbolic representation of the reality that the mind exists inside. When you take all the possibilities that exist, such as the decisions in your life, you will find that there is a major pattern that starts to emerge from your life. While it is true that the visual representation of time is in fact change, and that you are on a constantly changing path, and that nothing you see in the real world is actually the same from one second to the next. This ideology leads to millions of possibilities. If you take these possibilities and map them out appropriately, they create a triangular shape with a beginning and an end.

Beyond the barrier of the octahedron, there is an unknown amount of secondary octahedrons, just as you will understand how the null gradient exists and is present in the mind, similar to infinity. See the example of the octahedrons below, but imagine them spanning out to eternity. While there is a simple shape below, there would be octahedrons connected from all sides of this simple pattern.

It would, in fact, be repetitious with barriers at all sides. At the same time, the focus would be on the points, which exist on the objects. It is important as we venture further into this mindset that we adjust our mental picture of the way time moves in relation to a symbolic form of a linear line to the potential that it could flow from multiple points.

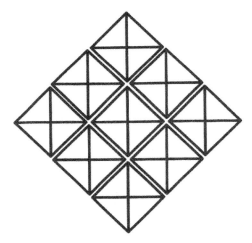

The Octahedrons symbolically encompasses the entirety of what is beyond the reality of the human experience. While this is just one set, imagine them connected in a giant pattern going to infinity on all sides. They are all connected via the 'chain' that goes through primary points on the pattern at a particular instance in time.

While this is indeed symbolic and representative of real-world knowledge of human-oriented perspective, there is a repetitious factor of a biological nature. There are patterns that emerge from the octahedron, and they can be seen in all physical objects around the world. As we look at the trees, the mountains, and the spirals that are everywhere, we see a consistent pattern of abstract mathematical shapes which create beautiful objects such as those found in geometry. They attempt to explain such visual topology, but it does not explain its hidden nature which can be initially obscured. While most organisms have a definitive reason for the type of shape they turn into, quite possibly due to a survival mechanism, there are shapes in the universe, such as a spiral galaxy (in a vortex), that have visual similarities to human DNA that are too close to argue that it is without purpose. There is a symmetry that scientists cannot argue against nor can it be a completely philosophical answer as science must use fact, reason, truth, and understanding to help the general populace understand this path.

It turns out that the repetition or symmetry can exist in the subjective mind, through the concept of ever-changing time and how we perceive our environment. We exist inside the shape that is similar to a tree as an entity on a path which passes through the octahedrons on an undefined relational route. For now, we see that the path is infused inside the octahedron and the shape that we are about to describe looks similar to the conception of the big bang, and the creation of the universe as it is known to the masses and the related scientific community. It begins at a point and has a gradient for a middle with limits and an ending. The key element to this set of octahedrons is that they interconnect with these gradients, and this is exactly how we think of the world.

Take for instance the triangle shape with the black gradient in the picture below, which for the dark part of it is symbolic of **null**, or nothing (the white part of it blends into the background so we consider it actual change). This is what interconnects the octahedrons, as they are combined. Null in this sense does in fact meeting nothingness, as Point A being the darkness relates to all negative possibilities or events that materialize from the null.

This is a symbolic representation of all null endpoints of the octahedron environment. This symbol shows that from one point we have nothingness, which leads to a small set of possibilities (the start of the white gradient), which leads to a middle of nearly infinite potential (the ending is a seemingly infinite ending, but is in fact finite) but this system is also limited by the possibilities that are not present at that time, making the unknown known again.

All of the understanding depends on your point of view and how willing you are to accept your visual context for where to begin with birth and end with death, which would extinguish that current visual representation from the human perspective. So, starting with the left of the symbol above, we move towards the right. This movement is just as we picture time to be, but imagining it from a three-dimensional perspective. So, in this sense, you would have an image of your head of a triangle symbol, but with darkness on one end, and sides at its points, existing as an object in time.

This can be imagined from the alternate perspective as well, depending on your view. For our purposes, we will focus on it from left to right with the one triangle to start with. Therefore, at Point A, we have the beginning of something in particular but not specific, which ultimately turns into endless possibilities. This can be true for most scenarios, but there is a limit as denoted by the lines, which encompass the gradient. The fact that the midpoint of the symbol (the image above) is finite is because there is indeed an ending to this particular point, but not specified in this example. There would be a secondary symbol to its right.

After we determine that almost any given octahedron has a beginning and an end, there is a middle portion which at a specific point in time is considered entirely full of possibilities, which is why this example expands in a fade, and if we were to closely look at the picture we would find a "chain" that looks very similar to a tree. If you were to replace the black gradient above with a chain of events starting with Point A, you would find a nearly infinite amount of options, which turns back to the example in question of the darkness, because of the completeness that exists in anything that has a flat color to it. Imagine lines instead of points or pixels, because in the real world there would be a seemingly infinite amount of potentials. When the options are symbolic and run in a certain sequence they can be thought of as a pattern, which is the case for this visual representation.

There are so many possibilities that we cannot have any clarity, which would be the same for a physical-based reality situation, in a visual and objective manner. However, we must know that there is a finite nature to this even if it is not in plain sight, which is why we provide just a simple example to start the process of explanation. It is important that we compare this shape to the octahedron, where at multiple angles we place the massive potential to be complex, which creates a solid when visualized at a higher-level due to density. This massive density creates the shape, even if it is abstract to the human mind.

To believe that null gradients exist at the sides of a symbolic octahedron is relevant because our worldview of the universe is very similar. When our minds imagine the concept of nothing (as in the opposite of something), it can be very difficult, if not impossible, for some people who do not already recognize what nothing could consist of. There are those that say that empty space exists beyond the universe or in those empty spaces, where most others would say impossibility is present. We could even replace the null fields with infinity and very well come up with the same outcome because these concepts in the mind actually reach a point of closure similar to the example, where the light of humanity starts and ends. Even if one imagines infinity in the mind, there is a restriction to it. Try it right now, and imagine what is beyond the universe, and go further with that and you will find that there is no way, because what exists beyond is not within our realm of comprehension, even if space were to fold back onto itself or become a loop, what is outside of the loop? There is some kind of ending that exists in the consciousness because it is as far as we can go in our minds, and therefore a boundary exists. For our purposes, we close the structure off and force the notion of a barrier because that is exactly where the mental projection of the human would end their thought process.

To enforce continued simplicity, we ask the question, "What is beyond the universe?" There are some that answer this question by stating that the universe is wrapped around at some convoluted dimensional substrate, but either way, the answer is always very complex and beyond the normal human perspective.

It turns out that the human being is not yet ready to answer such questions in our era due to the extremes that one must be willing to take the mind. It helps to have diagrams that help us understand the symbolic nature of our current world and to accept the idea knowing that we can only learn so much information. Later in this text, we will talk about what is necessary to transcend the model of the octahedron with technological progress or the similar symbolic nature that the human being is an entity that is constantly trying to learn the true nature of its own reality to go beyond.

THE OPERATIONAL JUNCTURE

Within the octahedron, there exists human nature and an approach that contains both positive and negative outcomes, all of which maintains a path of beginning to end. This is the chain of being for all decisions that were previously made on behalf of the currently existing human experience. It is at the current time, also known as the "here and now," which is called the **Operational Juncture** or opture for short. This is terminology that we find the real-time in the chain of events, where one point always begins, and another constantly ends. I also call the opture the **spark of life** because it is 'you' doing what you do in this time, at this point. It is a reference point that contains your current active life, your humanity that which contains the ability to be conscious during the time that is now. This terminology should be generally defined because when we refer to conscious it should mean having some semblance of life in it. For example: if you knew that the person standing beside you, was, in fact, you in another life; if you knew that in another life it was your mind—would you treat them any different? The you who exists at this time period is who you are at your opture.

This is a symbol for the opture which is the real-time stream of life that your consciousness perceives. It is the here and now as you are reading these words for the first time; it is when you read this **word**. When meditation tells you to focus on the here and now, this is the symbol for what they are referring to. When you think about each human life and sentient being having a 'soul' or energy that keeps them alive, this is the system that is being referred to. In that sense, each consciousness utilizes some kind of awareness.

We sometimes forget that our friends and neighbors have an essence or consciousness to their life, they think as we do, maybe not 'like' we do as they may have different views, but it is essential that we understand that they see out of their eyes and can hear just like we do. Let's not forget about animals such as cat and dogs. While they do not possess the same intelligence as humans, they are alive and have a spark of life that should be respected. They are the **others** or those who are not us and can easily be neglected because they do not exist in our current mind (i.e. their reality, we can't be two people at once so we don't see their viewpoint exactly).

Our world would be much different if we were all interconnected at the same time, this way we would understand the importance of a human life. We are able to see out of our eyes and utilize the operational juncture which does, in fact, allow us to continue on our journey. It is at this point that we need to know that without a doubt, **understanding our journey in a negative frame of mind is an impossible task, but understanding through positive thoughts increases the probability of success.**

The opture is a reference point that has a future and continues to create new memories on a daily basis in the mind of the human. Therefore, the opture is, in fact, a snapshot of a currently existing moment in time that is constantly changing. It is never the same and is always different, providing a visual context to the constantly changing reality. This is the essence of time itself from the human perspective, as it is indeed changing, moment by moment.

This is also the 'real' time frame of the observer, and now knowing this we can accept that every change prior to the opture was just the change leading up to the point you are currently living in. At various points on the opture, your frame of reference will move faster or slower, which is based on activity or the type of moment. This movement or change that takes place during the opture is the **chain**.

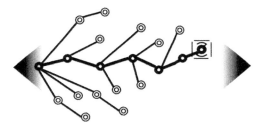

This is a symbolic representation of the 'chain,' which starts with the universal point A. At the start has multiple and seemingly infinite amounts of points that it can relate to; for our visual example, we only drew a few points. As change progresses along the path of choice, we end up picking a path, ultimately leading to the end. To the right of the image is the null gradient, same with the left, both show birth and death. At the end of the chain is real-time, or the here and now.

The chain is contained within the realm of time where movement is constantly taking place in the octahedron. The element of the cause or the first event (this can also be referenced as birth, not just the first event of the creation of reality) created this and all chains, which initialized action to a **parallel grouping** of perspective.

This type of grouping is shown in the example, as objects similar to branches stem from the primary chain. It was the first action that created this chain, and to us, this is known as **birth**. Depending on your point in the chain you will find that there are two first causes: Point A being the cause of the first events of reality, and Point B being the birth of the human or your inherent reality. This second cause is the one you know to be the truth because you live it on a daily basis.

Obviously, the normal consciousness is unaware of this because of the baseline experience and of the limits we have. What is infinite is currently beyond human comprehension in the active sense, and what could have caused event A is unknown. The creation of reality and concepts beyond the norm can be experienced by the human mind but forgotten shortly thereafter because we are not yet capable of containing such an excessive amount of information. It is possible that with the development of advanced technology, we may be able to contain such life experiences.

We can only know the limit of what our brains are capable of at this point in time, and know that beyond the barrier exists a chain of events that links our current consciousness to the beginning of where the individual became the word known as 'coherent.' This is also what is meant by the universal mind that understands its current state of awareness. This is where technological progress comes in, and the possibility of transcendence with assistive technologies, but for now we must focus on the framework itself and the knowledge gleaned from the logic in place all while making helpful observations along the way.

This action-taking place at the current opture of human perception is also considered the **participant** or quite simply, your life at the moment of time that is right now. While we have focused on this concept quite a bit, you must also realize that you are taking 'part' in a reality. You are the conscious entity or the personal-internal that can transcend through the external realities of your daily life as the minutes pass by. As you look at the other humans around you, they consist of substance in their own space, but only for that instant. It is through the internal and external substance (the barrier) after the initialization factor of birth takes place that allocation begins, and the journey of the participant from many different perspectives occur. This happens in a finite span of time, and the experiences of the observer become apparent from within the subjective mind.

This execution of events continues to be known as a 'chain' which consists of events in other octahedrons, from an undefined path as mentioned previously. The human needs directly fall into the category of what causes the chain to continue on its path, as the external becomes internal, the human calms the wave of change of time in between the limits of both positive and negative. It is, in fact, possible to exist in reality because of what happened before you were born as the events that you cannot see in front of you and potentially events that will not happen due to causes of your own. During a finite amount of time your life was determined before you had a chance to even take action, and these actions created you by the will of not only the others but the determinate actions in life.

The chain does appear to be infinite with regard to its container (the primary octahedron) but is really limited with a large capacity. The number of decisions is therefore finite, and there are top and bottom limits to these decisions that the chain consists of. In our minds, these limits form the geometrical pattern of the octahedron. Your essence of life was created by the chain, as it is universal. In this timeline, you had no decisions that you could have even made at the point of your birth. You were born into a system that was not of your choosing. At the same time, you developed an awareness that there is indeed something different about the world which is not immediately recognizable. This may be considered a gift or a curse depending on your overall outlook about human nature. It should be about the chain and the will of a human being, which exists in the system, the network of changes that allows you to exist at this moment in your opture.

There is also the **threshold** system which occurs when an action is repeated until change is forced to occur. Many actions in this world and many decisions have a threshold where a 'breaking point' starts to exist and a decision that was once simple or possibly complex is changed into something completely different. It could also mean that an action reaches a point of discovery or goal, based on what a person has aimed to achieve. For example, if we want to obtain value out of something we purchase, such as a car, it might be to our best interest to do regular maintenance on the vehicle so we get our investment from the original purchase. However, some decisions may take place prior to this threshold, which gives the concept two different types of terms. First, the **primary objective**, which is the perspective when a final point of discovery completely changes beyond its original intention. Then, the **secondary objective** is the personal goal to make the object continue to appear brand new while meeting the **primary threshold,** which is the point in existence of something we consider to be perfect, that exists within the octahedron. When objects are utilized, they are changed by the movement of time, which initiates a threshold.

Another example of thresholds is edible food or perishables. As it is a need, it is limited in its availability which forces humans to come up with new ways to sustain themselves. The universe has made it so that we have objects in our environment that we can ingest to give us nutrition. In nature, we can make the decision, when it is ready and meets the threshold, to eat the food or we can choose to throw it out. Most likely, we will not throw it out because of the amount of time it took to make this object from a seed in nature. It is essential that we view this world from this perspective because everything has a value; it's just a matter of what actions we have taken to increase production so that the time it takes between creation and consumption is not only limited but has the most utilization. There is a perfect point in time at which the product can be ingested, the perfect primary threshold, and the same goes for other points on the chain. Throughout the chain, this is a major part of our decision-making process, because we initiate an event, but in the end, there may be different results due to the thresholds.

When understanding the universal mind, we find that it is all-encompassing because it contains all parts to whatever exists at that point in time as it does at the operational juncture. There is a beginning, middle, and end. There are origins in universal objects. At each turn of events, there are so many alternate paths that exist on the chain, but there is only one actual true path that the mind follows. If there were no universals, or constants throughout time and space, there would be no beginning and end. The amount of change that takes place would be infinite, so we must remember that the chain is part of time itself, infused with the universal mind. Time is the perception of action which is deeply connected to everyday consciousness and its connection to the world you currently exist in. We sometimes lack the words to describe this as it makes up your mind and body. Your brain is constantly trying to make sense of all that exists around you and how to better interact with the objects and people in your environment. It has been thousands of years that human beings or the molecules that make up them have been attempting to determine their true purpose. You are made up of this energy which can now look upon itself in a critical manner.

This is part of the reason that you exist in your opture as you and not in a different opture as somebody else. The reference point is you and it could not be any other way in that instant where you question your reality and remember that moment. You exist as a human being in the body that was provided to you from the chain of events that existed long before your birth but at this point in time. We do not remember being born and was not a decision on the chain to enforce prior events, so we have to accept that some decisions were made for us in this reality. However, in a different octahedron that exists as an infinite construct, at a different point in the chain of this particular octahedron, there would be an instance where you are somebody else entirely. It is made even more complicated by the statement that "you are everybody" and that you actually exist as the person beside you and anything else that has an opture.

No matter what action in your life, the questioning will be constant and sometimes even cause you to lose touch with what is important because you ignore the fact that everything around you has life in it. Your confusion is entirely understandable; this confusion can cause anxiety because you must constantly attempt to understand the world around you, as the interactions build daily with questions you cannot possibly answer as you see the time pass by and your world changes within what feels like seconds.

It is an evolutionary approach on a mass scale and can be mostly explained by science primarily at the more detailed levels. Part of the big picture is that your consciousness is the chaos, constantly trying to make sense of it all. Time has caused overall existence to happen, which for us starts out as the base experience, and leads to a turn of events where we are all alive, but in different optures. The chaotic nature of the chain is because it wants to create and maintain, but unfortunately, there is no 'order' without the universal mind in existence. The universal mind is the person you want to be, with the knowledge to move forward in a world where you have control over your own life. This is where the daily struggle comes into play, and there is the force of change fighting us for the next course of action, the events that make sense at that moment for time.

We are at war with time in this sense. We are constantly trying to fight it with all of our might, and this causes great fear of the future. This fear is primarily about death which in and of itself is a type of awakening, or a motivator to perform a particular action in life. It is a very important part of life for the person performing an activity, and most likely give the drive to continue moving through change. When humans possess the knowledge that someday they will no longer exist, it changes their motivation to a massive degree; but what happens when they ignore this motivator and do not possess the understanding that their time is limited? In the chain, death would result in the chain collapsing at that particular instance. Time needs to force the entity to continue on a chain that leads further into a second, then a third, and fourth, and fifth Octahedron, to potential infinity. It is through this example that we would have two possibilities, the first would either give us life after death in a different form, without knowledge of our current events, but only after all opture potentials have been completed. The second option is nonexistence or the darkness of nothing which would be implied if we exist only as brains in the physical world of our current general environment of logic.

Review the image below, which is an attempt at visualizing the octahedron (the two-dimensional model) and the mass amount of decisions contained in the chain, and the geometrical pattern that it creates. In this sense, we can use this same logic that deters us on occasion to a form that points to substance beyond the internal. For our purposes, this is key to understanding the reality of the octahedron.

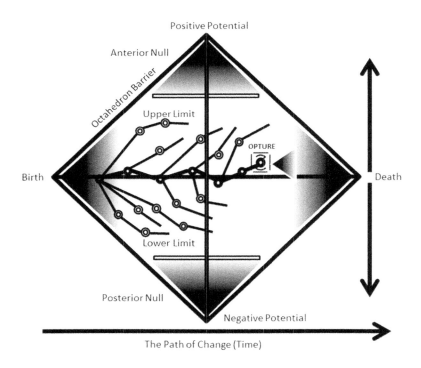

This is the continued representation of the octahedron environment, however, the null gradients are included that show the journey of time with the 'chain' and its constructs. Birth and death are shown with the both positive and negative potential. Most importantly, the **opture** is shown, which is the real-time here and now.

As you can see, the process begins with a general overview of the barrier that is the octahedron. The simplification of its constructs can be accomplished by building a framework; this is something we are attempting to do in this text. Then, we cross the middle ground of knowledge and perception which employs the chain of events as they progress towards the big picture. Time caused the perception of action, which is cause and effect, as well as the action itself or the perception of action. It is circular to state that action caused itself, but in this case, we see that as humans are the internals to the octahedron, we lack the ability to describe this concept fully or understand even our limitations. In addition, we are limited by the human brain itself as it requires technological assistance for complete infusion into this framework. Complete understanding of the mind and its connection to time will take years to resolve. This leads to the realization that beyond one object exists another larger object.

This is very similar to the Russian Matryoshka doll which has another doll inside, and then another, and another; but in our example, we have the universe which shrinks down to clusters of stars, then the Milky Way galaxy, and then our solar system, then our Earth, and then to the human. This chain ultimately leads to our minds. Beyond this is the world of the atom which is a whole other world in and of itself. This idea that systems are inside or outside the other is called **internal/external grouping** and is different from **parallel grouping** which is when alternate decisions exist on the chain, existing side by side as a tree as we talked about earlier.

Then, through the internal/external grouping, there is the personal internal, which leads to the social internal. An example of this is when the external transcends to the internal and when the molecules and atoms provide definition and substance, which allocates itself to the journey of the participant, the viewpoint that was created from the extended chain as it continues along the opture. All events prior to the being are considered secondary events after the opture. Through this, there are necessary requirements of living a human life that has caused this movement throughout time; these include air, shelter, food, and knowing threats about our surrounding environment. This internal environment also includes the categories of truth from the human perspective, to make the right decisions in the face of uncertainty.

The human being, the active mind attempts to calm the wave, and slow down time with the 'right' decisions or point the direction of the chain to another point in time where life is easier, but this does not always work, and this is the reason for subjective analysis. Even if we knew what action to take for the greater good of the self, we would still affect others in ways we cannot even imagine. Just as you exist because of events prior to your birth, we unknowingly follow these actions because that is a framework to the octahedron. It is through the universal mind that you can make the condition equal and full of order, instead of erratic and chaotic.

In this sense, you are the participant. Regardless of how you feel about this, you were created from the chain and time is your container. You could say, "I am" or "I exist," but you are here as a person, part of the chain. We're all here; we exist plainly, with many consequences of our own actions. It is ideal to realize that a possible purpose is to prove that we are born to interface with a technological environment, which would consequently lead to the connection of the opture, to what is beyond the limit of human understanding. The chaotic nature of the chain is that it wants to create and maintain. As time moves on, humans will continue to develop new ideas and concepts that they did not have previously.

Advanced interaction with technological progress will create awareness that we were previously unaware of and will continue to be part of the universal paradigm shift of the human race, where we transcend all known barriers.

THE FEAR OF DEATH

To be afraid of something does not necessarily mean that it will be actively present in daily life. It does not always refer to something that is immediate in the mind. While greatly ignored in the conscious mind for the most part, the fear of the death is indeed present in the culture at every turn. No matter where we go as humans, who we meet, or the experiences we have; there will be a fear in the back of the mind itching to get out.

It is persistent in its cause, forcing us to constantly examine a world where we no longer exist. It is a strong motivator to perform an activity that you would not normally do. People say to themselves, "Well, I can't take it with me!" when they want to spend money or hear of a funeral and then concern themselves with the idea that their day will come. Not existing is something we all fear because it goes against everything we know as humans. Our whole existence is life.

This is not to be morbid or to bring more darkness to the text nor is it written in a negative sense. This work has the intention to help another person reach a state of mind where they understand their true self, and in order to do this, we must know why we act the way we do. The fear of death is a strong motivator to act a certain way, and it's commonly ignored as a reason for an action. We are afraid of death and not willing to accept death, but that certainly does not mean that someday it will not happen. It is our nature as fragile human beings to pass on. We can actually recognize that the days are limited, and any experience we seek to enjoy should be completed in this life.

We cannot know what is beyond life at this point, and we do not want to accept this unknown factor. As a result of this failure to accept and a completely understand death, we form multiple systems to deal with it. An example of this is that we distance ourselves from the event as much as possible. Not only do we allow those that are in their time to pass with the peace they deserve, but we also try to allow time for goodbye. At the same time, the human does not want to see the act for it is confusion and disorientation, for as to actually see death and not distance oneself from it, we are reminding ourselves how real it actually is in this finite world.

We do everything possible to try and rationalize the death that is in front of us, and tell ourselves so many stories to make it fit the norm, and we also do this to hide it from those we care about and allow ourselves to exist in a world where we do in fact ignore it on a daily basis. At some point, the fear seeps through the mind and presents itself in multiple ways. The distances we go to try to escape death are in fact drastic, putting forth effort that would not normally be present.

The most common way that we see fear and act on it is through religion, as the fear of the death becomes associated with the ultimate unknown or what is beyond life itself. Having a spiritual entity in the mind, with the true belief that we will survive death greatly enhances the justification for a religious system, and forces the individual to accept a behavior that they might not normally have taken part in the first place. Religion comes from many points of view, and some of these points include communities of people that have developed their systems of thought over many years.

The sociological implications are that humans sometimes use these rituals to justify actions, sometimes good and bad. Obviously, not all people are like this, but the point is that we should look at our own actions and determine if they are relevant to our continued development. Physical or geographic locations are also considered spiritual in some religions, as faith has a way of giving a human the belief in a higher power. It's not so much an external source forcing the person as it is an internal justification. The justification goes beyond logic, and those humans who are more susceptible to the suggestions would be more likely to follow through with the action in question, but not because they were unable, forced, or coerced, but because they feel that the action brings them closer to understanding. There are peaceful religions and violent religions, but that is not the point which is that your actions along the chain enable you to make the right decisions but it is up to you to recognize the difference between right and wrong.

This is not to say that those who follow a religion are vulnerable. Almost the entire population of humans has a belief in a higher power, and not all of them would jump off a bridge if told to do so. It's important that we understand this distinction between science and belief, because when people are serious about their spirituality, they are in fact using some kind of logic to determine why they feel a certain way. Ultimately, we want to assume that the primary reason for the religious point of view is possibly because of the fear of death and the potential for an afterlife.

When a relatively normal human being makes the decision to believe in a force that is beyond him or her, it's usually because they have a fear in the back of their mind or question about what is beyond the realm of the living. They have questions about what could be beyond the rational, wondering if they will have a place in the afterlife. There are also people who are born into religious households or those that grow up in an environment where they are taken to the religious location with their family on certain days, but this is slightly different because the educated decision to be 'religious' or 'spiritual' isn't actually present yet in the human mind. It takes years to actually be responsible for yourself or make a final decision on where you want to be in life. In this sense, they have not yet made the decision, their family has.

It appears that what we gain out of this writing is understanding that when we look beyond into the future of our lives, we see that we can either spend our lives worrying about the end, or we can start living our lives in hopes of a better tomorrow. There are times when we can look to the future and maybe we will realize that sooner or later the end will be near, but we can't spend our lives chained to the idea that we will somehow cheat death. This is where spiritual insight becomes important to our lives, as it gives us a way to accept that someday we will in fact die. It is indeed practical to think that all action in our lives revolves around our fear of death and what will happen in the years to come, but it is also relevant to work on resolution of a method by which your mind can be at ease with this notion because the fear will retain itself unless you take action to accept it or learn to ignore the thoughts and negativity that comes through the mind. Keep in mind that we cannot ignore these truths of the world so in this sense we should focus on acceptance.

PRACTICAL APPLICATIONS

The key to utilizing this chapter to its fullest extent is being able to distinguish the daily activities and experiences that happen to you. The "here and now" is the most important point that we focus on because it is the active life, the Opture which is the result of the past, and the actions which determine the future. This is the point where your senses are active, and the visual representation of the world exists at its highest point.

That is the focus of the opture symbol as its sole purpose is to force you to recognize where you are at this point in time and to see change occurring right before your eyes. This reminds you of the life you currently live, the decisions you make, and the people you influence. This is where the senses take action, as when you actively use your mind to perform activities. What you may think and what is really going on around you are two different things. The mind is obscure in this, and sometimes feeds us incorrect information about our world and those around us. It is through our world of social interaction, the internal and external groupings where we find social constructs and sometimes our perception of people should be questioned as it may be negative for no good reason.

Having awareness of your current thoughts is essential to understanding the thought patterns you seek to change. Another example of this is through meditation and breathing. Positive affirmations and recognizing the change you seek to make are essential during this phase. If you are involved in a routine such as work or study, then take time out to focus on the self.

This way, you can find happiness in the moment and learn to appreciate the good things that happen to you. If you are in a bad situation where you feel that positive affirmations are not working, then a plan must be executed to escape that current environment. It is essentially this simple, as your life can, in fact, be changed with a single event.

The symbolic system is indeed a major part of our analysis because it directly relates to the system of the Octahedron. While it is, in fact, symbolic and in very few ways is visible to our immediate senses, we should focus on going beyond the norm to understand this point of view. The new era is focused on technology, and the human race is continuing to strive for some kind of perfection with technology (such as computers), which leaves us with the conclusion that maybe someday we will look back on our world and see that innovation was the direct result of repetition, forcing us to see the true nature of who and what we are as culture expands.

Finally, accepting that someday you will not exist is another factor that most of us don't even want to have in our minds, it is a negative force but one that must be confronted. The inspiration that we find in the world around us can be a solution to some of these negative issues as we must take the time to control our thoughts and desires to enhance positive beliefs, which can lead to amazing outcomes.

The best action to take for this is to work hard in your life to become healthy and attempt to extend your life. If this is not possible, then know it is not the end by any means. We have no proof of an afterlife, but one can speak from a faith based system and know that even if there is nothing, something existed at one point, and know in your heart that the energy that exists as 'you' must transform. You are here, now at this point in time and space, utilizing the current motion of time. In the end, this means everything. So now, take a moment to breathe the air.

Actions and Thoughts:

- Know the reality of 'theory' and the importance of understanding topics that go beyond the norm.

- Learn what it means to be ethical and do the 'right' thing.

- Ask yourself the hard questions like, "Why am I me and not somebody else?" or "Why was I born in this era and not a different time?" These questions bring about a positive mental change which initiates the 'theory-mind' and forces you to think critically as well as abstractly.

- Change something in your life that makes you feel bad.

- Learn the symbolic system of the octahedron, its paths, and representation.

- Recognize the chain of events that led to your birth and up to the present moment (the Operational Juncture). Look around you at the events currently taking place and where they could lead.

- Look at yourself as a **spark of life**, and question its existence appropriately. See beyond that which has been named.

4

TECHNOLOGY

A s you continue on the journey to the second reality of the universal mind, there is an essential piece of knowledge that you must comprehend. The key concept that we cover in this section is technology and its place in our world. This part of the theory is about the quest for knowledge and power through assistive technology or Artificial Intelligence (AI); these types of advancements keep you connected to the Internet and continuous mobile device development. These concepts force the very essence of your personal identity to be driven further into new experiences and sometimes assist you in life with your problems.

The technology is likely to take you to places that you have never been before, and will most likely allow you to encounter new experiences that are special or can make your life easier to some extent. Many people need to wonder if the technology they carry is actually special because of the help it provides, or if it is because somebody with market power made them believe in the product or unknowingly forced them to look at it in an interesting way. This is just one of the simplified questions that we ask regarding our perception of technological progress by constantly looking at it from an external point of view.

Sometimes financial gain and societal power from those that control the mass populace influence the technological ideology. We know that humans are obsessed with technology because of what it can do with regard to making life easier and more interesting. Many years ago, technology hit a point of exponential growth, becoming more advanced. The need for a more specific or intelligent object came to the minds of our species so that we could make larger changes as well as more precise decisions. It is hard to say exactly when this change occurred. Those that originally created the first computer network with the intention of sharing knowledge may have had a large part in this paradigm shift.

Many years after the start of the intentional massive destruction of the wilderness for the purposes of expansion without cause the humans hit a point of growth with technological machines that could calculate numbers, all as an extension of the mind. The human was enthralled with anything that he or she could not do. From a professional work perspective, when the groups gather for meetings each person competes for the best results, sometimes ignoring the end goal. Ultimately, we did not mean to destroy the trees or the wilderness, and it is not that humans do not find it beautiful. It is just that it does not fit into our idea of the perfect society. The issue is that we have worked together on a system with those in positions of power, to establish a system that forces us to comply with the destruction of our earth.

Then, of course, with the concrete cities building up over the years, the technological network of information (i.e. Internet) was in fact originally designed for the purpose of communication for military usages; it was useful for those reasons. In the process, this technology paved the way for so much more with regard to personal communications. Along the chain of the octahedron, it could be argued that we had no choice because it's possible that all technology is being developed for the purpose of connecting the opture.

It was at this point, the human could sit in a chair, interface with an object that could interface with another human, or they could have a wealth of knowledge at their fingertips. It is important to note that every technology ever built will have the ultimate purpose of making communication between humans faster, more precise, and realistic. It may not seem so at first, but if we look at the trend over time, we will see a mass expansion of the 'interconnection' between the minds of humans, which stems from this development of mass computer networks.

The initiative also allowed some humans to capitalize on the endeavor, and they found it to be worth the initial investment of time and money. Development of such products is interesting for that reason, because you cannot know the value of a project until its completion; you can make an educated guess and plan accordingly, but the more difficult the project, the harder it becomes to predict the outcome.

Beyond the financial-based issues, there is one very important point: we are constantly assessing personal improvement even if we are unaware of it in the beginning. The value we gain from new technology ultimately pushes humankind in the right direction. It is where hope and inspiration come into the big picture. Technology can save humanity from disaster, as long as we use its concepts in a relevant manner, and according to the views and ethical considerations of the general population.

The most hopeful future in the eyes of a human is one with space travel and leaving our planet to visit other or solar systems that support life. To go beyond Earth really is the ultimate goal. This journey is something that the Earth is preparing a path for so that humans may make the right decisions along the chain to leave the planet. The key point we need to address is that yes, humans are destructive, but we are a result of the Earth and its creations, so in a way, this path may be relevant no matter how inconsistent it sounds. It turns out that space exploration may be our key to survival. As a major element of humanity, may be the point of human existence is to leave the Earth because we are running out of resources and getting closer and closer to our own extinction.

We know that humans have fought each other since the beginning of logical thought. In this book, we attempt to answer some of the questions such as why, but the point is that in this technological reality we must make plans to leave the Earth at some point in the near future or we will most likely be unable to survive. Nevertheless, for some reason, we as humans cannot seem to get to that level of understanding. We tend to forget about what is above us and focus on existing at a base level where there is only the norm. The topics of existence and time cannot be forgotten. Knowing that the goal of humanity is to transcend the mind and body and possibly colonize other planets until we reach a point where technology can support our human form.

The idea that we can move beyond the Earth is essential to where we are on the path of discovery, especially if we are unsure of the exact future of the fragile human form. As a human, we have a beginning, middle, and end which all occurs in the mind when we picture where the human race actually is with regard to progress and how we will be in the future. If the society you are living in is not moving towards the ultimate goal of space travel, then you should ask yourself the question, "How important are we at this point in time that we are not striving to achieve this goal?" It is not that we are going to abandon the planet; it is that we cannot sustain this level of living for an extended period of time.

No matter what type of scenario takes place, there is a situational understanding in the mind of the observer where fear and the motivation to recognize that our days here are indeed limited, and just about any deviation in our normal human days could result in disaster. For the long term, we must strive to accept the certainty of the future, because our human lifespan needs to utilize all available methods to go beyond where we are, and as humans our goals are not complex; we just have hopes from a basic perspective, but unfortunately this is not enough to plan for the future that is in store for humanity. An example is right in front of us: we breathe oxygen amongst billions of people on an Earth that is extremely limited, that is in a vortex through the galaxy at unbelievable speeds. All of us enclosed within a thin atmosphere that protects us from a deep, desolate, cold, and dangerous space environment.

On Earth, the long-term usage of technology can perform amazing outcomes, and technology can even outperform a human in some respects. However, this is also 'virtual' and has not been accomplished outside of the computer hardware and software. This is the point of using the term virtual in the terminology – the technology will, in fact, outperform the human, but does not replace the human.

Think of the work involved with forcing you to purchase a piece of technology, then think about the symbolism drawing you closer to it. It appears to be part of something so much greater than ourselves which we do not immediately notice. That is where symbolism strikes a chord in our mind.

Those that market technology have selling down to a science. They are willing to do whatever it takes to get the product in your hands and the money in their hands, yet they do not harness the power of new technology and limit it to the consumer for the purpose of long-term financial gain. We have all been in the position of wanting something new. As humans, we follow the symbols like lost sheep because like our ancestors we enjoy the aesthetics and artistic essence; in our era, we have phones that would have never been imaged years prior, objects that we can appreciate and that can assist us in all aspects of communication.

We have to ask ourselves, is mass communication phase one of a much greater plan such as interconnection of minds, and are we just waiting for phase two to occur? Many companies and people choose to exploit technology, thinking that if they can own one of these amazing technologies they have what is needed for the new standard. A simple example of this standard that we find to be an amazing 'new' technology is a smartphone, and now the smartwatch. In some respects, ownership of a smartphone is required to live a normal life as you need it to purchase products or check personal information. The technological processes, rational, behavior, and ethical scenarios need to be re-examined because in our era the progress that has been made can proceed with both positive and negative consequences to the subjective and objective populace.

To examine the technical details of such scenarios may not be enough to show you the damage that is actually being done to the society, specifically with regard to privacy and individuality. Regardless of where we are headed, the inquisitive nature of the human should always have the need to ask the important questions. This is a primary objective of looking at your subjective self, knowing that without a doubt and at all times you can stop and think about who and where you are in your life, and where you are going to be. It is true that we do try to keep the text on track with the subjective point of view and examining the internal processes that exist in your mind to the external environment that you interact with. Occasionally, we may drift into similar territory where the connections are deeply rooted in knowledge and the acquisition of power which directly correlate with those that control the technology and what they can do with the products in question.

The technology is surpassing humans to the point where human identity and compassion is becoming less and less important. We have to wonder if the 'normal' human considers the actions of creating entire cities and reproducing beyond the means of the populace as ethical and if creating products and ideas that end up being negative as a good idea. We go beyond the ethical implications because of the animal instincts that exist inside, the 'survival' traits. To develop new technology, it is in the mind of individuals with the vision to go beyond the norm, to present views to the external observers, and follow strict scientific guidelines to enhance their own cause.

To some extent, when we talk about cities and urban environments, it is indeed a selfish activity to advance technology the way we have done it because the inventions can completely remove rational thought from the person utilizing the technology. The technological process is very complex, but when we talk about cities, they were not there in the times before the human. The forests and trees existed, and as the humans reproduced, more and more trees were removed from the ground to create massive boxes and 'clean' surfaces that do not, by any means, resemble the dirt that was there before. It is our obsession with clean, smooth substances that force us to tear down old buildings and place new ones there and destroy the remainder of the forests that exist on the Earth.

Because of this, humans are now limited to the public property that we've created for ourselves and we have gone ahead limited our grasp of the environment, per individual. To a certain extent, we are only allowed on grounds that we permit ourselves to be on, living by our own rules and our own laws which in fact restrict us, and by this we could be domesticated in a sense that roaming free upon the land is no longer an option. Could we conclude that technology forced us to do this? Not as a separate entity, because technology is the internal-external, that which we utilize to assist us in all matters. The technology is a major part of our lives and the way we develop objects of interest either for personal or financial gain.

The path we took as humans from living in the forest to actual modern-day houses has been a long journey. Technology has been the solution to a great majority of the changes that have taken place for the end result of us living in relative comfort. You can only imagine what it was like for the first humans; they did not have the luxuries of the modern era, and daily life was exhausting and took a great deal of energy to work without the technology that we know they did not have at an earlier point in time.

A certain lifestyle must be lived from the beginning, as a human is born into the world where they will adapt to and live in permanently until their death. As we live, will utilize the technological process during our time, but to have any clue to what these concepts are we would need to go camping but not just to the nearest forest that is governed by our laws. To reproduce this life as it was, we would need to do some sort of primitive camping, but with strict consistency. It would be very difficult to even closely reproduce (in our era) what it was like to live in ancient times. At this point, we would need to go back to what we call the 'baseline' of humanity, at least try to imagine such a place. It is the starting point of civilization, and this world is where we begin our technological journey with the creation of objects that have assisted us throughout time.

The actions of the person who takes part in the creation of an object can complete a positive or negative activity for the group that is utilizing this object. If this person uses technology to perform a negative action, then it can turn around and do the same to him or her. At a point after the user is numb to the effects, he or she will accept the negativity—and unintentionally cause harm to others. Therefore, these technological objects of development often lend themselves to the external observer's unintended consequences more often than not, sometimes for purposes other than which the object was originally intended.

The technological progress can sometimes be the end-all of an individual or group of people. They will sometimes force themselves to utilize a particular technology to gain notoriety or power beyond that particular system of thought. This 'silicon ego' comes from both men and women who work in the Information Technology industry. Over time, the human becomes numb to all actions performed in the work environment. This can also happen in one's personal life, but it takes much longer to completely adapt. The same goes for an absolute change, as a human will have great difficulties separating him or herself from the technology in question and will go to great lengths to be rude to those in the group who do not conform to the base standard of the technology in question.

An example of this is when a society of half modern individuals with technology or people who involved with, utilize it and plan with it, and half tree-dwellers who do not utilize technology, push forward in time through an evolutionary process. What will the two groups look like?

The question comes up repeatedly of whether or not the part of society with the technology will be superior to those without the technology. It could be said that this question may not even be relevant because those who possess the technology will surpass those without it, and within a number of years those who are lacking the advanced methods will no longer exist in the same environment, possibly because they have moved on or are no longer in the same domain of knowledge.

It is not apparent at first, but the idea that we are the technology we seek is a far-reaching concept that might first stumble in the minds of those who do not recognize the timeline of the human and his or her technology. They walk hand in hand. When there is a need, there is a human who has a solution or multiple humans with similar ideas always willing to put forth the effort to make life easier, sometimes even at the expense of others.

After all these years, we have developed a network of machines that are almost capable of assisting the human in transcending the current physical mind as we exist. At this time, we are unable to completely duplicate the mind, so artificial intelligence as we see in popular fiction is most likely not possible. The AI we see now will be present in the software, assisting us with our daily activities, which is exactly how it begins. In time, the AI will gain ground with the humans and surpass the norm. When the human brain can be duplicated, there will be another great paradigm shift, one that finally gives permanent assistance to the human's needs.

The ontological argument of artificial life and advanced knowledge of human awareness, or how we could someday communicate or infuse our environment with artificially intelligent life, is enough to put the mind at the edge of a terrible perspective. The result of such an advancement could be horrifying depending upon the sequence of actions that occurs during the actual change. When in communication with such artificial intelligence, the words of subjectivity, existence, and non-existence would have to be examined in detail, even though we may not like what we hear. It is then, that we may be forced to deal with the new objects that we have created on some unfortunate basis.

Humans demand neat and artistic products that produce some kind of pop-culture influence, forcing the value of other objects to rise as the manufacturers and related parties continue to acquire wealth, utilizing sometimes-unconventional methods. It's key to our comprehension that we realize that once the wrong product comes along, users may have to re-examine their outlook on life, especially if the products are utilizing technology in a way that puts humans in a surveillance state which endangers our privacy or becomes so subjective that it infiltrates our personality even on a social level.

Once again, the question comes up about AI and the ability to find a relevant interface for the artificial life to learn from. This learning platform could, in fact, be the cameras and microphones we love to put in everything to record our lives. Currently, in our era, we have developed a method of retrieval which is video recording, and some may see this as a bad thing when it comes to artificial intelligence, even though for us it can be a good thing when we take video of our lives to look back upon.

The object of our discussion, in this case, is artificial intelligence, which from multiple perspectives can be thought of as a byproduct of the industrial era. The uninformed say AI is "a machine that is conscious," but this is not yet the case. The definition in this sense is important because humans are in absolute denial about what a real artificial intelligence could in fact be; the 'deliverable' of an AI is not some robot (but it can be).

Instead, we should imagine a very horrible and terrifying organic machine (that may look like a human). The size of the AI object in question would depend upon the era and level of technological advancement made by the humans that created it. Yes, it could, in fact, be humanoid, but it could also be connected to an output device, such as a simple screen or projection.

The questions we have to ask ourselves in the sense of the

subjective mind which deal specifically with the question of, "Do we upload ourselves to this device?" or "Is this machine conscious of its own will?"

ARTIFICIAL INTELLIGENCE

The birth of a new era and the artificially intelligent 'species' or 'types' will emerge. They will most likely be in a controlled environment where the birth factor will come into question as a highly advanced brain would need a body in order to be considered complete. There will indeed be a degree of personal continuity present in advanced artificially intelligent systems which will include perceptual awareness of knowledge, reasoning, and communication. These traits will be compared with human cognition derived from neurological processes. There are, however, inquiries regarding human individuality that will be adhered to which are not effectively present in the materialist perspective.

From this perspective, we can assume that the machine will become self-aware as we have: of its own development and by using its pre-programmed state to derive knowledge from the surrounding environment. This happens over a certain number of self-directed evolutionary intervals; we can assume that this organic mechanism would then develop its own personal continuity.

While there are so many arguments presented from a philosophical perspective regarding artificial life being metaphysical constructs, we can derive that the machines will have 'knowledge' similar to us and that we can, from the machine's perspective, draw conclusions therein.

We can initiate valuable premises about the judgments about possible human personal continuity with regard to our consciousness being replicated onto a mechanical device. Regardless of these philosophical implications, we can derive new logical rules and proofs that would govern such definition in artificial intelligence. As with any complex system, there are rules that take place to govern the mechanical apparatus that is to become self-aware and develop a personal identity. The two most fundamental instances are the material with which the device is made and the algorithms present in the 'mind' of the device. Then there would be a timely interval which takes place in order for this machine to replicate knowledge. This is possible if we utilize modern technology to enhance the authenticity of the learning methods and the visual representation that we seek.

The human cognition factors and the combination of a killing instrument would make for a deadly weapon indeed. It all depends on how we utilize this material. Either way, we take this situational approach where there are pros and cons which need to be addressed accordingly. How the system itself learns, replicates, and relates to the local or global environment will all depend on its initial programming: conceptual analysis, linguistics, mental representation of objects, ethics in the machine, value-based creation, and how we observe objects in the environment.

Then we need to determine how the mind of the artificial intelligence feels about us and how would it 'feel' to recognize that we are so much more flawed than it is; and then upon its realization of its superiority, what would happen? There are various difficulties that arise when developing a general distinction between the initial creation of an idea and how self-understanding puts an objective view (of one subjective mind) into another observers consciousness, so in this case, the external observer is an artificially intelligent life form. The point we are making is that we still cannot, with absolute certainty, say to ourselves, "I know this reality because I see it through another person." The creative consciousness that you possess would somehow need to take part in the logical behavior, to create objects of importance based on the memories of the being that we consider unreal.

The categorization that occurs to the artificial being is, at its finest, a doctrine of the digital philosophy of the mind which ultimately will play a dramatic and possibly devastating part to the continuing struggle of human existence. The key point that we are making is that since we, in fact, do not know ourselves, it is highly doubtful that the machine would know itself. It is possible to create intelligent AI, but there must be the mechanism for reproduction engineered into its entirety.

The machine must be capable of utilizing the correct thoughts, and then putting the correct actions in sequence on a finalized product. This would apply for both mental and physical precepts. One would argue that there is AI in some products, but these are connected to a memory chip or a speaker and most likely contained in plastic and connected wirelessly to the Internet which makes it severely limited. Now, if the AI in question was a secondary device to a primary, more advanced AI, it would be considered a device for gathering information.

To completely understand this reality of AI and the internal nature of the self which is essential to understanding how technological advancements relate to that part of your mind, you need to completely know the subject matter. Some would say that it is your absolute duty as a human being to take part in any endeavor which allows us to transcend the normal behavior, to advancement by either goals or behavior, which ends in newly-created or recreated objects.

The objects in question are the technology we hold in our hands or the lights we stare at on a regular basis. The key to this amazing, intricate, and complex system is value-based creation which means that no matter what you do, you will always seek out a better method to complete a task and bask in the glory of your discovery even if it is for the worst.

It is when the objects are created for financial gain that those involved start to have desires to facilitate a particular task that could either be good or evil. An overused example of a negative technological task is the development of nuclear weapons that have the intention of protecting a nation but can also lead to the ultimate destruction of a valuable Earth species. This system inevitably leads to **mutually assured destruction**—which keeps the peace out of fear for now. In this effort, you find the much talked about the will of the human and his or her drive to survive.

The will to create is acquired through the origins covered earlier during the development of the human, and we talk about it when referring to the chain. You are born with the need to use your will, to survive, and to extend the lifespan of you and your species which contains some of the origins of the actual development of primary and secondary technologies.

Beyond the interest in creating an object of implicit design in the operational juncture, we do find a need to assist some of our leaders for the common good of the masses, who can sometimes lead humans to technological advancements for the wrong reasons.

It is up to us to look at the timeline of technology and realize that there are various stages of development in the span of technological progress. The process begins with an attempt to solve a problem that is presented to the human in a certain way, stumping the human and making them look inward. Typically, this is out of a relevant need, and, therefore, the invention process begins.

After the human has designed a method that works to solve the problem at hand, it is indeed very difficult to force the clock back to a time before the technology existed. To do so would involve removing the knowledge that needed to begin with, and causing a great deal of pain for those that have lived the life the technology provided. Once an idea has been documented and exists in the mind, it can spread and constantly move forward through the masses. Moving forward will result in the peak of that particular technological process, most likely with a different technology replacing the previous one. In this sense, the timeline of creative development is extremely important when we look at the ingenuity and creative behavior that has led to such amazing advancements. This forces us to ask questions such as, "Where do the ideas come from at all?" or, "Are they borrowed from others to enhance the greater good, or do we just continuously follow the chain along our path?"

Therefore, the speed of human adaptation to particular technologies is essential to the consumption of the products mentioned above, and it is this same time frame which is also directly related to how a human interfaces with the machine. The social structure of the masses must utilize the technology with some kind of interface. At the beginning, users start out by slowly testing the technology, and it goes through the rigors of time, but in our current era, the factor of time has been cut down with advances is in rapid development.

The social classes have pushed for the acceleration of production factors in our current cultural environment. We lack certain time frames to properly test products so instead, we have a society of testers who live on the new products and sometimes become dependent on them. This is essential when talking about the role global cities will play in the future as the point of progression can only go so far where all users are testing the same product for a short amount of time, and the product, consumer, and manufacturer are working at high-speed rates.

The human race isn't ready for the speed at which this technology is being applied. Some humans on our planet have absolutely no final goal or end in mind with regard to the value-based creation or where they want to be in the future. Either way, it's valuable for all humans to ask the question "Is the goal to use the technology to leave Earth?"

To determine the next step is the always the key element in the vast array of questions and views one human can offer another, but this is lacking in our era with human desires and the suffering it creates over financial objects. It's about "me first, you next" too many people, where they are not focused on others well-being, but only on themselves. There are many who believe that the power is in the actual knowledge when, in reality, it is with those who know what to do with the knowledge.

All of this leads to something different. **A new type of computer**—which must go beyond us. The machine must go through human development, finding existence at the end of a birth, life, and death. The machine must be able to tap into that spark of life that exists in a human being. This device will not be something we now know of as a device. It may exist as an "object" but not of the binary system that current technology we utilize exists in. Instead, it will compare to that of the finely tuned instance, where knowledge of its existence will force a change that our eyes have not yet witnessed.

PRACTICAL APPLICATIONS

To move forward with technology means that you must be willing to accept you might lose control over your life at its current juncture, so in this sense you must not lose the control you do have. There are multiple points that must be made with regard to taking control of this instance. It may not always be easy to do, but we must push forward through the uncertainty and fall into line with the possibility that technology is an assistive partner to the human that we should continue to utilize.

The first human beings utilized technology as a means of survival, and we now use it to help us in our daily lives. It is everywhere we look. There are multiple categories of technology that you can learn about, and how they each impact your life in a certain way. Especially now, we find technology that relates to health, agriculture, transportation, input/output, architecture, electronics, energy, information, and much more. Prior to this era, there were only a few options for technological discoveries but over the years this has changed greatly.

For us to define technology, we need to look at the objects that already exist in the world. We could say that technology is a change in a primary object over a specific length of time that enhances the secondary object in question. When a conscious observer utilizes technology, they enhance their experience and focus on a forward movement toward new objects of interest that may be more relevant for that particular point in time. Obviously, we want to make our lives better and live in a peaceful world where we can be safe; technology is used very often for this purpose.

It may be difficult for some people to accept the fact that they will at some point need to interface with technology that they may find so complex. However, there are some who already are highly experienced with the technology as they can manipulate data to transform their ideas into reality.

Actions and Thoughts:

- Ask yourself, "What is Technology, and how does it work?"

- See Technology as 'assistive' and determine how it's useful for you.

- What is the goal of Technology?

- What does the 'baseline' of humanity look like, and how can you experience it?

- How can you help nature and the earth to prevent its destruction?

- Realize the importance of Artificial Intelligence (AI).

- Think about what a new type of computer would act like, one that exists beyond the binary codes we have now.

- Take some time away from Technology and go out into nature.

5

UNION

The union is the third reality; this is where you find a connection between humans, or as the operational juncture is concerned, you will find the other side of your life chain and the unity that is required to sustain happiness at some level that is sufficient. This is a specific type of connection that reaches us on a higher level of the mind, as there are many beginnings and many endings to this experience, and it can pass as quickly as it began. This is not an experience that one just creates or replicates from example. While it is, in fact, a physical and justifiable experience which should be relatively easy to explain, it's just not simple to explain.

There are many types of unions, but we will first focus on the most familiar. When a person falls in love with another, they find that their entire mindset changes which include their conscious decisions and memories of events. This is not necessarily a negative action, and the intention is to focus the direction outward so that one can control the moment and find something that is known where there was once something unknown. The union of love is one of the most important concepts of coexistence in the octahedron and movement of the operational juncture, as it amplifies the decisions that are made in your life. If you are two instead of one and the both of you agree on decisions, then you are that much more powerful when it comes to survival. This experience happens when you least expect it, and you may not even realize what you actually had until the other person is gone. But by chance, you may end up living in a union until your last breath. It is up to that particular chain of events and what direction they are expected to go.

Not only does union refer to the distance between two or more people, but the connection that is established between them. Union itself is a need and is part of our survival as human beings. Humans have an interest in group-think or being a part of a team where they can contribute accordingly. Without getting into the psychological aspects of the social landscape, we can agree that union is required for the mind to make a connection to another mind through a form of communication like language. Therefore, it is beneficial to acquire education and have abilities such as public speaking or skills in non-verbal communication.

Either way, it is important that the decisions you make with unions synchronize with your overall life goals, and during general observations of personal hopes and dreams, you will indeed find surprising results. Love and kindness are some of the most important human experiences that you can have. If you have had it in your life consider yourself very lucky. Never forget to take the experiences with you as best as possible and never forget the times you have had because they may be the best in your life. If this is not the case, then you may have learned from the experiences. Even in friendship, humans can learn the value of the connection between two or more people.

You must remember that it's possible that you only get to live one time here on Earth. This is entirely relevant when it comes to thinking about a missed opportunity to be with the one you love for any amount of time. This is what we think in our heads; we imagine how important it is to spend every waking minute with this other person of whom we are in love with, or at least romanticize of what it would be like. There are general guidelines to the human experience when it comes to this type of union. Generally accepted ways humans look for relationships are based on age, interests, and more depending on the situation. We have to keep in mind that this is just one part of the 'union' reality, as there are several different types of unions. The purpose is to understand that there is a connection to the opture among humans that force communication which goes beyond talking about the weather with somebody on the street.

The union between people does not always have to be romantic as there are friendships as well. The relationship in the mind is based on physical, spiritual, and biological traits, but we cannot rule out the possibility of a non-physical substance, or metaphysical view that entails this relationship. The union in this sense maintains attachment, affection, and kindness. Marriage is one of the most popular and common unions that take place in the world. It is a vow that we do not just speak but live in our daily lives for those that have had the experience will understand. Those that have not yet experienced it will find themselves on a path towards something truly amazing.

We initiate some unions by being kind to others or showing some kind of interest. However, only through working on ourselves to improve our interactions with others will we be able to make relevant connections. Some unions take place between people who have very little interaction, and some people question how this is even possible that two people with few common interests can get along so well. This can be done in many ways but is primarily done through understanding another person's point of view. It is important to note that memories make a person who they are and one cannot be expected to go back and change memories that already exist; therefore, they cannot be expected to change the personality of the other person. Only new memories can be created with a human being, but new memories sometimes can replace old, bad memories with a more positive outlook on life.

When we speak of union with social networks and the Internet, creating new memories in a group of individuals is extremely complex. We already know that the general purpose of individuals is to continue the species of humans as best as possible. With the population increasing, we have indeed accomplished this task for the moment. However, when we combine this with technology, a complete change occurs in the process. Over time, there is a transformation of the human potential that was not present before. There is a great amount science involved in social networks, and it is not our goal to focus on these levels of complexity, but rather the small portions of the real-world relationships that take place.

RELATIONSHIPS

The initial phase of a relationship is usually a general connection with another person. There is a mental and sometimes physical connection that depends on the level of interest and compatibility. Union in this sense refers to the relationship with the purpose of reproduction or continuing the species. This kind of meeting can now happen on the Internet without any prior in-person interaction, leaving out some of the steps usually involved. This process now involves a 'filtering' of the people that you could be compatible with during a frame of time.

Sometimes we cannot filter out the people we meet in the natural environment. They seem to randomly occur in our lives, without any prior meaning. The professional work environment is not normally a place where we would meet a significant other, however, this does happen from time to time. As stated, in our era the initial process is completed via the Internet, and then the second act of filtering occurs as a date or dinner, which can sometimes be a longer span of time depending upon how well each person wants to ask questions and learn about the other person, this is also how likeminded the union is, in hopes of continued connections. This is the typical romantic relationship process, and to contrast this to the friendship level experience which would include general types of activities.

The human relationship itself can be difficult to describe when it comes to the types that are not romantic. This is where love differs, as the concept has its completely own system of thought. When one person loves another, it is completely different than a personal friendship, business relationship, or business contract. It's important that we distinguish between these different categories because some may argue that love includes friendship, or friendship can include love, and to some extent they are correct. But for our purposes, we are trying to show that there exists a communication that is mind-to-mind. Some may agree that with the Internet, we have separated people and made it difficult for actual social interaction. To some extent, we have just made it more specific.

The relationship will grow from its initial interaction and after complete acceptance, each person will attempt to make a final agreement to grow the connection from a baseline. As any human social construct is deciphered, we find at the opture the primary and secondary needs are fulfilled by utilizing the union that has been established. While we will not get into this level of detail, we will say that usually the primary focus is to find food or shelter for the secondary. It is important to note that the primary can be either male or female. The same goes for the secondary. This purpose will change as the relationship builds to new levels. Some tasks may become more appropriate for one or the other.

In time, the relationship will end. This will be the result of choice, an unavoidable circumstance, or death. This major change occurs in friendships as well. In time, actions occur that cannot be avoided as the movement of time forces all things to change. Once again, the purpose of this is a sincere and obvious connection between people, for increasing the value of human experience. To recongize the connection between people, we must also understand the disconnect or where the entire process ceases to exist as this is just as important to self-discovery.

THE SOCIAL GROUP

Being in a relationship is the first stage of developing a social network. As your connection with other people grows, you establish a foundation for future survival. At this point, you should have the necessary experience to enhance the nonverbal contract between the people involved. It is important that you always follow the laws of your nation should they prove to be fair and always perform just and ethical actions. All of these methods go back to our ancestors, in that some human beings were not social because they didn't have to be at the time. Maybe they wandered through the wilderness and were completely self-sufficient, where the more social humans would work with others in trading for necessity.

Being in a relationship forces you to depend on others for goals and milestones that require teams of people. These relationships can cause issues depending on the size of the group, their training, experience, and expertise in general. If actions can be done independently, then they should be. The team should only be utilized when needed. The goal in mind may be attainable, but we have to determine if it is necessary to bring in others because they may want to share in the attainment of whatever objects are acquired. There are those who engage in competition, forcing others to take part in activities that would determine their skill level to not only gain their trust but gain their will power. This type of activity takes place primarily in the workplace but can happen in social groups outside of the workplace. Fulfillment and development of the situation also possess a level of competition that can be fierce when a leader's respect is involved, especially with regard to rewards and what can be obtained from winning.

At their base level, humans can be very animal-like in a sense that they lose all humanity when it comes to games of a social variety.

Obviously, the game depends on the level of interaction, but even the simplest games can entice a human to fall victim to a negative interaction. It's seen time and time again where the 'system' in question grabs a person's wit and expertise, forcing them to desire a portion of the end result, never letting up until completion. In our society, winning really is a great deal of our daily routine even with simple tasks. The reason for this is usually present in the mind due to a lack of control elsewhere in life. This isn't to say the weak mind takes part in games; it's sometimes the smartest of humans that play games for rewards.

The network of individuals must learn to respect each other, to forgive and forget, to understand and comprehend, but most importantly attempt to see through each other's eyes. It is a part of the chain to know that, in time, you could be the other person you seek to inflict your interests on whether they are good or bad.

PRACTICAL APPLICATIONS

Being independent and having the ability to reach your goals or milestones is key to this chapter. As well, understanding what it means to love another human is key to this chapter. Communication between humans is essential to the development of a relationship and is practical in a sense that you must utilize the greater good to obtain a goal. You should take time out for family and friends to establish a baseline of communication. The purpose of all these concepts within a union is to enrich the mind of the observer and to develop the overall concept of the group experience.

Actions and Thoughts:

- Learn to filter out unreliable information and utilize that which is important. At the same time, don't neglect those who have been positive in the past.

- It's important to have a union that is either a romantic relationship or a friendship. Develop your network of friends within reason.

- Focus on the outcome of the relationship and how it can achieve the greater good.

- Recognize when you are in competition and determine how best to serve others instead of struggling to win a resource. Learn to share resources, also within reason.

- Understand the connection between technology and union. It's important that we utilize technology to create a union, but at the same time, we utilize unions through technology.

6

THE WORKER

T he fourth and most mentally and physically challenging reality that we face is our existence as the worker. Sometimes this can be related to a being a warrior or fighter. The path of the worker is usually through a career or work-oriented environment that is human-created. This is a major part of being on the path of action after related theories of reality have been acquired.

I combine the two concepts of work and war in this sense because being a warrior or a fighter requires a great deal of actual work. Being a worker requires a person to fight or battle in one situation or another either in the short or long term in no particular intensity. The two concepts are interconnected because if you want to be successful at one, then you must take part in the other. There are different paths that can be followed in this sense: For example, if you work hard to find employment, then continue on the path of the employed professional, you in some traditional sense are a fighter. There are many instances that regular workers would

139

consider themselves 'at war' even though they are not even close to it. No matter what place in life, you will have to work at some point, and it is important that you understand that this is part of a major action that takes place.

Then, all of the actual actions will depend on your field of work, and what you do for a living. I know that a soldier in the military is not the same as working in a cubicle as they are different environments. In comparison, both will have different experiences. However, beyond the experience factor, looking from this from the objective point of view, one must become a fighter to be successful in the corporate or public service work environment.

In an earlier chapter, you would have found that people are always thinking about themselves, or following the "me first, you next" philosophy as it is up to you to realize that there are very few people in the world who will give up their own selfish need to help others. The interesting thing about it is that when they do actually perform an activity, it is for selfish reasons. Ultimately, they are still performing the good act for the benefit of themselves, even if they do not receive anything in return but the mental gratification.

To be human in the world of today means to take part in an environment that is considered the term 'professional,' or part of the societal change that involves many humans contributing to an activity that benefits the other for financial gain. The term itself means that one would typically acquire monetary objects from performing a skill or using some kind of knowledge to help another human. This type of work has officially taken over the world in developed areas where technology is prevalent.

Throughout all of the angst, frustration, and work that is done, humans have found ways to make the world a better place through work. In this sense, the action involved is centralized on a particular perspective of an individual. It is about equalizing the world to a certain degree and forcing each other to follow a set of standards known as the law. Enforcing the law, as it is in our modern culture, sets the standard of moderation whereby all humans must follow similar paths as if they were tamed to not utilize the now dormant animal instincts.

Those that follow the norm of modern culture and maintain employment with a company are considered to be suited to work in an environment that directly correlates with their education and experience. This is usually the case in the hiring process as a person will not be hired for a position unless they are qualified, which leads to the continued self-inquiry, but this isn't always the case. It is up to the human to enter into positions where they can excel and gain recognition, ultimately to acquire monetary objects.

How the human performs this activity is up to them and should be done in an ethical manner. It is important that we review the potentials that take place when we talk about the control a human has on another human, objectively and subjectively. The hunger a human being has cannot be taken lightly as it is essential for the person to eat, breathe, sleep, and follow the basic needs we discussed earlier. The position of employment and control vector takes this into consideration, which leads to control, but for our purposes, we should focus on the delusions that take place in the mind of the subjective observer.

We can only imagine what it was like in ancient times for the human when appetite was no longer a concern or how the human would work with the group to decide how they would plan for their next meal. A majority of this time was used for planning and developing ways to survive after the needs were fulfilled and when all urges were satisfied, this is typically when technology and innovation became more relevant. We can assume that humans of this time did, in fact, get 'bored' and would resort to planning and working in order to keep busy. Part of the reason that a majority of humans work so hard and do what they do, which is to prevent the act of doing nothing, or being nothing. A human who has nothing to do with their time is considered to be wasting their time. This is not to say that a person who is doing nothing is a waste, but to themselves, they will be without value internally if action is not taken.

Therefore, throughout the ages, even if the act was simple or obscure, it was still better than doing nothing. It became apparent, that beyond hunger a human must find goals to occupy their time, and they must find actions to perform in order to fulfill their purpose. It is in this spirit that we find humans who want to utilize technology perform the tasks that were once considered new and exciting, but now menial and boring. It is in this world that we see technology taking the mass of our jobs away, and forcing us to be innovative.

HUMAN HUNGER

Before office life, it appears that such a career path wouldn't have been a reality because we hunted animals and foraged for food but would spend less time doing this than the hours we spend in an office or a cubicle to earn finances for the day. However, before the current era, the wilderness was dangerous because it was home to its original inhabitants, the animals that are now going extinct. Over time, we destroyed that environment to create our own. This process is not yet complete as the human race continues to fulfill its desire to build and develop foundations in hopes of continued expansion.

The most important difference in this activity is the amount of continuity that has been established, and the amount that can be gained from the modern workday. To kill an animal requires a certain degree of hunger that cannot be achieved in our modern era by the man or woman in the western world; only in certain circumstances can a human in today's world be 'starving.' Typically, only those in financially unstable countries have the unfortunate effect of starving, but it is true that anybody can go hungry, at any point in time.

Humans that are actually starving are put in a position of absolute terror and it can be assumed that for the most part, they are on the verge of dying from lack of nutrition. This leads to the absolute necessity or bringing out the **action-internal**, the human animal instincts. Now, in our current time, not all humans have to deal with this, and Earth actually contains more than enough food for all humans. However, it is currently in the wrong hands as some people continue to make it impossible for equal nourishment to occur.

As it turns out, the combination of a survival instinct, a large family, sociological constructs, and time all cause some individuals to have more food or 'food potential' than others. It is not their fault, it is not our fault, and it is not your fault—right now at least. It is the fault of those before us in the long span of time that is the human experience, or the 'chain' of existence. While you do not want to take the blame, maybe it is in our best interest to stop assigning blame and start taking action.

Your type of employment and the way you live your life is out of absolute necessity, and it can be assumed that a good portion of the population gives their fair share to those in need. Unfortunately, it is not enough to give a small amount because it does not guarantee that all humans will perform the same activity unless they have incentive. The purpose of you going to work on a daily basis is so you can acquire the monetary objects you need to allocate your resources effectively in the new system, to have proper shelter, eat food, drink water, and fulfill the proper needs.

Along with these needs come the great delusions that make us believe we need amenities such as the shopping malls that continue to feed the machine that is corporate greed. There are countless examples of this in the world, and we do not to have look far or be a conspiracy theorist, to find them in the real world. There are those that do not want to accept the truth that a majority of the life we currently live is a necessary delusion. The world you live in comes from an idea that somebody else made up to gain monetary objects.

I want to be clear and state that this isn't about the homeless on the street trying to get the occasional dollar which sometimes adds up to a decent yearly income. We are not looking for a solution for hunger or feeding the poor. The leaders who maintain one percent of the wealth must make these changes; they must give up what they hold most dear, and it must be out of their own accord. Regardless of the method by which humans work on a daily basis, we need to understand the entire purpose for why a person performs these actions, and more specifically look at the daily routine to understand the truth of our environment. For the homeless, hunger and work are completely connected. This is about survival and control, two very important topics that directly relate to your humanity and where you want to be in your life.

The top percent of the population who own a majority of the financial objects (man-made and virtual) on Earth give those of us who are less fortunate a way to have a 'career' so that we may work in hopes of achieving the same level of success. This dream of allocation goes for college education as well, which was designed to allow a younger human of lesser knowledge and possibly lower class (based on the system the powerful have developed) to accumulate debt by which they would gain a degree (paper contract) that would allow them entry to a job after they completed rigorous study and proved themselves worthy. Beyond the multifaceted complexities of the system we now call law or government, we find a very simple idea of control.

Yes, actual people run the government. There is not some organization such as the Illuminati or other secret society that runs the entire world from a circular table. However, there are certain groups of people that have a great deal of power and can, in fact, steer changes in a specific direction with the right amount of influence. This is where the law fails society. The law of man has its limitations, and they exist when putting beside the power that money has over another human.

It comes down to the fact that people have no idea what they want in life because most weren't taught to want the right objects, but the downside is that they believe they are not wrong. All humans are driving in one direction which can sometimes be viewed as "me first, you next." This, in and of itself, is based off each human fighting to obtain the best possible outcome with the best possible financial objective. If we want to know how things should be in this world to enhance our quality of life, then an attempt should be made to look to the future and recognize that actions should be performed a certain way.

Without the rule of law there can be no order, but when humans go beyond the rule of self-governance, the law starts to become fiction. We sometimes lack laws for this type of behavior; when the human is hungry for more, we have to decide what will happen.

THE CONTROL

This control we speak of is headed in the wrong direction as some people push their beliefs and views upon those with little or no education. This causes the 'educated individuals,' out of pure ignorance, to perform actions they would not normally do as they are provided with financial objects or forced to do so by other means. This causes not only one person but also multiple people to hold onto a belief system that continues throughout a person's life; they start to forget about the true nature of why they started working, to begin with. Some even become addicted to the lifestyle of the common 'workaholic.'

This is especially true if they start at a younger age as it will be more ingrained in their psyche from repetition. We are creatures of habit, as it has been said. Humans have, over time, been taught or forced to do the same activity repeatedly with little deviation regardless of internal feelings.

Human beings are in general very lazy; they want to do less and gain more. They believe they are the only people that think these thoughts when it turns out all of us are after the same objects. This is where financial objects come in as they do at most times; they are the ultimate motivator because they provide you with the ability to gain something when you normally wouldn't be able to. But there is a situational perspective that happens when another attempts to control us. It is important that as you develop your future, you turn to the past in presenting yourself. Look at who you used to be as a person, and force that future self to adhere to what the past neglected. In this sense, you should force yourself to say or do the things you would not normally.

It is one thing to be dedicated, motivated, and constantly striving to help those in need such as those on your team or in your family. You need to focus on the life that you are living and the regrets you will have you are deathbed and say, "I wish I hadn't worked so much." This does not imply that you should quit your job or start working less than you committed, but you should be spending the time you have outside of work on tasks that will get you out of the situation that made you unhappy to begin with such as the repetition that you are currently in.

Obviously, you put yourself in the position to make money for a reason. There was some type of gain that you acquired from all of this, but it is time to reassess where you currently are in your life. This is the faith that takes place when accepting that there is an activity that you are supposed to be performing that you excel at, but are not currently doing for financial objects. Sometimes people say that you should never forget about what you have, but I like to think that if you forget about what you have and think you have less, you will appreciate what you have more. Maybe then you would be thankful. This is not always the case for those in positions of power and control.

Those who wish to control your life occasionally work in teams. Sometimes the size of the team varies, but either way, they are working towards a similar goal and it is up to you to understand and recognize that there is a team being formed. The speed at which they work in the contract is also important because, like I said before, it's about time. Whoever controls the amount of time you have, and how often they obtain monetary objects, is who has the greatest value in the contract.

The work you do is about automation, continuously developing a working model that has the best outcome for those who helped create it in the first place. The people who own the contract also have the same issues as those in the contract, of not realizing what is already in their possession. Because the work you do is about automation and causing the money to come in at an advanced pace and go to those involved with the financial objects, an internal goal that is sometimes nullified by the delusional self who wants nothing more than the shiny new red sports car, or the house that is beyond the current financial objects you are currently bringing in. That is the problem, curbing the urges that come from the animal self that is continuously taking advantage of by others.

Think about this in the long term. Focus on human life as a whole. It is in the long term that we can really determine the needs of the populace and how technology itself may or may not resolve the issue of us having our tasks completed for us. A human is interesting in this sense. He or she wants something to do with their time, tries to find ways to eliminate menial tasks, but then gets sick of it and forces technology to automate it, then repeats the process.

The problem with this situation is that we reach a threshold where the human will be forced out of the picture, and technology will begin automating the tasks that are required for the human. This is where the artificial intelligence conversation overlaps greatly. What happens when there is no more relevant employment for humans and when the machines have taken over? This would most definitely be unintentional, but through the perpetual change and advancement that humans have to make there will most definitely be a change in the world that leads to artificial life. The time for when this occurs is uncertain, but for the human who wants to understand our world, now has to contend with the technology that they are connected to on a daily basis.

THE CONTRACT

You are currently restricted. Your life and everything you do is placed in a container and limited by those fellow humans around you. You gave them permission to do it for the greater good of the world. The reason you did this was that there is not just one of you, there are billions. The other humans are just like you; they are animals. Given the chance, many would take what you have either by word or by force.

That is why we have laws because a human being without laws is in a state of absolute chaos. Therefore, the more humans that exist in the world, the more restrictions will be created. The empowerment that was given to assist one another will be concentrated, interpreted, and escalated at so many different points in your life. You will ask yourself how it is possible that we reached this point.

A majority of humans go through life assuming that they are somehow more important than those around them, that they are entitled to an object that some other person actually has in their possession at that point in time. People continuously assume this fallacy because the objects are still all within the boundaries that we have created.

The restriction is about importance. Now, humans may not be able to just flat out take another's possessions due to the rule of law, but that doesn't keep them from believing that they are not equal and somehow above one another in one way or another. Humans are all flawed. At our core we make mistakes. Depending on the situation, these mistakes can be a good thing or they can be our undoing. This is where the rule of law and the set of standards come in which do not always account for the real world.

What you encompass is what you create, it is your container and the restrictions for you and your family. This is especially true if you have had more children than the norm because in that case, you are contributing to the overpopulation that is taking place in the world, but it is, of course, our absolute right to have children, the concern is how well you teach them to communicate with the rule of law. Of course, some countries are not increasing in population, but overall the humans on this world will be over almost 9 billion people in less than 20 years, which forces all of us to ask the hard questions like, "How is this sustainable?" This line of questioning goes back to those in power who have to make the decisions for you because you gave them the ability to do so, and without them, we would not have the laws.

It is extremely cyclical, the system that the humans have created, and the reason that this was done is that it is built into our consciousness, to have a leader, to follow another human, to follow a repetition, to survive, and, most importantly, to fear death. It is sometimes through these other humans that repetition begins to build, which can sometimes be difficult. This depends on the type of work you do. When dealing with other humans during the action phase, this is called the **contract**. The use of the contract implies the use of monetary objects. There are many different types of contracts that exist. The normal terminology does imply truth; however, it does not assume that the contract is needed for relevant communication. What we are saying is that when any sort of exchange occurs that is non-violent, casual, or relevant to the object, there has been a contract agreed upon. Sometimes this contract does not always present itself immediately, or at all, but it's there.

Different types of work in our lives will produce different levels of comfort. It is appropriate to assume that the more education you have in our society directly correlates with the type of work you do. This sometimes implies the amount of work you do and therefore comfort level. Some people think that it is in their 'cards' or was because of who they are currently that they have wound up in the position that they are currently in today.

This control that comes from understanding who you are and where you want to be is peace of mind that you will definitely want to possess. Fortunately for you who are reading this, you can work on the contracts that life throws at you and develop your own personal contract with life, one that gives you the advantage. You have to weigh the pros and cons of your actions and make sense of what is right or wrong; this is the true action, the way to make a serious difference in our world.

CORE SELF

You are developing a method right now as you read this book, and you started prior to picking it up. There are core levels to understanding yourself. These exist even in the work world. Sometimes in our lives, we find ourselves searching for something greater than we do. A meaning that we seek almost always has a purpose or reason and starts with the core self. This is where the action takes place.

During the path of action, we must take part in a journey that will allow us to perform activities that can be considered either good or bad. Just as in any part of life, we gain experience and become more valuable. Those who have gained more experience are definitely more valuable, because they are able to predict what may happen, and utilize memories that may have occurred previously for the greater good of the team. The outcome then would be so much more inclined to be more effective, which relates to the work environment as well.

Overall, the world of professional employment may seem difficult for the core self as it is a daily occurrence where the individual must strive and push beyond the norm. As the days fly by, the core self unintentionally ignores the secondary aspects of life that were once primary. This in and of itself can be an issue depending upon what the activities were, such as social or educational activities which are typically the first to be ignored.

Usually, the constructive work environment tries to emphasize the importance of education in the workplace, and the appropriate environment will allow this to thrive. Unfortunately, the employment system is about obtaining financial objects, so the needs of the core self can be left out. Having the contract to do the work and achieve the desired financial objects can motivate the self and fulfill some needs, but it is not enough on the spectrum of human importance.

PRACTICAL APPLICATIONS

The first thing you want to do with your professional career is create an action plan on paper. This should consist of where you are currently, where you want to be, and how you will get there. If you are unsure of how to get to this future goal, then you must seek out assistance. In this sense, you should know the ways professionals speak, what they do in their spare time, and what type of people they really are. This is called 'work talk' or the way people act when they exist in the professional environment.

This way of communication seeps into the normal world as some people bring their work home with them, and they can sometimes become a different person. The subjective nature that was the individual can be taken over by the objective career focus even in the off-hours when this was not to be expected. The personal focus can become anxiety ridden, and the human who was once in charge of their mind can become lost within the goals of the company that is now in contract with them. This is once again part of gaining experience. The goal should be to work in moderation, focus on coexisting in this environment until an alternative solution is met or by working on a contract that is in the best interest from the beginning.

A general strategy must exist at this point where you can initiate a foundation for future growth. This development program is the essence of how you will gain experience in the industry that you have chosen. Ultimately, recognizing your end goal would be the ideal point to be at in this instance. Understanding, and creating your own passage of time in the mind or a virtual chain where the mind can force the physical body to go, which leads to success for the subjective mind. Some people who force real change to happen in their mind can take the world and its constructs way too seriously and start to enforce the little control they have on others to some extent. It's important that we plan to protect against this type of behavior from others, but maintain the understanding that this happens because of the need for financial objects and greed for more. Emotions can run high, especially in the work environment, but this is partially because we are at the baseline, animals. Humans were originally in larger environments such as the forest, which is much different than a cubicle area.

Actions and Thoughts:

- Work in a field or profession that you enjoy and learn how to get to that place.

- What are the needs of a human and how do they pertain to being a professional?

- Understand the objects of desire and financial independence.

- Learn how a 'contract' works with another human.

- Know the core self and how valuable experience is in the world.

- Schedule time appropriately. This includes focusing on the self and the goals to enhance your quality of life.

- Develop goals and have an action plan.

7

UNIVERSAL MIND

T he fifth reality begins at a point in time where all actions have aligned and you become one with your core being. It may feel like a random point in time, but it is not. This change in your life will feel as if you have reached amazing potential, beyond all circumstances and with the odds against you. Through time, you have worked through the theory and action. Now, you are ready for a change. This is your awakening where all the prior actions or knowledge in your life led up to a point of real utilization. This is real change, and this is really living. Finally, you have worked your way through the cycle, but to continue the success, this cycle must be repeated.

This is at a time when you have achieved some semblance of what spiritualists would call enlightenment. It is at this point that your reality somewhat shifts to a perspective that's clear and concise, allowing you to understand what it all means at least for a brief instant. A person is not meant to 'live' in enlightenment; this is something that you experience for a short to moderate amount of time without the use of any mind-altering substances as true enlightenment is utilized with the base self. The term itself has been used negatively in a sense that those under the influence of a substance would experience altered states of reality from chemical induction. The use of an unnatural foreign substance to induce a high-level state will not encourage a level of advanced perception. Only by natural methods can a human achieve true perspective. It will then be inherent in the mind for future use to the subjective mind.

You are different chemically from the person you originally were when you were born, throughout the time your body and mind have adjusted to the decisions you have made, making you complete in the way that you have defined. Achieving this point of view where you can recognize the actions you have taken and the actions that led to this point is essential to realizing not only who you are as a person but also who you are going to be in the future.

You do not have to be a perfect person in every way to achieve this level of expertise with regard to the changes. The strangeness of reality will soon be present. What is even stranger is that you may not realize you have achieved the ultimate goal until after some time, when you look back on the combination of events. It is at this point that you find that you knew the action; you were, in fact, knowledgeable of the logic involved. Unknown to you at the time, you were highly skilled when others were not. Prior to this, you will know that time passes so fast, so completely, that memories of such an experience may be blurred, to be not as real as they once were at the opture. Just as the time it takes you to read these words passes by, or the time it took you to achieve an amazing act.

We are the universal mind; we are the atoms that surround the all-encompassing nature of reality. Any scientific phenomena that we can think of can somehow be linked to the knowledge that is present in a human being. So, in time, we may be forced to transcend this Earth, utilizing the technology that we have developed, to go into space as the cosmic mind. In this sense, Earth is indeed a spaceship that is traveling in a vortex, on a path to a destination far away that is completely unknown to us other than through stories about travelers that may go to space in the future. We, as humans, can find many reasons to be here, but it is now that you need to make yourself aware of the world around you, and the changes you have made, are making, and will make. All of the world is waiting for your changes as you learn the theory, perform the action, and make the change.

The opture that you are at currently is enhanced using technology, and in time you will encounter many new usages for these devices.

While it is true that we are at war with time and the changes it induces, it emphasizes a deterministic view of the world, forcing us to realize where we want to be at this time and in this place. The goal is, in fact, to break free, to have the will, and force change that would not normally exist. As time was not meant to force the determinism on our world, we exist as the chaos that enhances our mind to the 'universal' state which transcends the norm, allowing existence for itself in a different chain of events that time did not intend, as this is the purpose of the universal mind.

This is the symbol of the self. It represents multiple points and ways of movement. This is the symbol of the universal mind. One person is the same as all people. It does not matter what race you are; it is the symbol for the human and has a specific meaning. From the symbol above we have two triangles, the top triangle represents the heavens or the sky above, the bottom triangle the below, or the negative nature, with the lines in the middle being our Earth. The triangle itself is a symbolic reminder of the Octahedron that we exist in.

As the universal thinker, your first objective is to be ethical. Included in this, you have to follow the rule of law. It is important that we distinguish between societal law and universal law as well. Universal law being actions that take part across all societies. Just as prior sections in this book provided you with the problems and countless issues with the world around you, this section will give you a fighting chance at solving the same problems by utilizing your internal talents.

You need to help others; it is important that if you have the capability to do the right thing that you, in fact, do it. Do not let time pass you by without performing the correct action when you know in your heart and mind that it is, in fact, the ethical decision for that particular dilemma. Work to go beyond the negative behavior that may prevent you from developing your mind to its fullest extent. The complexities involved with historical accounts of ethics and making the 'right' decision are numerous, as the general opinion is that human nature is mostly good, but has a bad side.

Instead, I insist that you meditate on the issue. I hope you are not one of the few who have had negative experiences in the past which have forced you to constantly make the wrong decisions in your life. Are you the one who makes the wrong decision and forces others to suffer? If you have not made the decision yet, then you are not necessarily the one to blame. The process that has amplified your negativity is to blame for the chain of events leading up to this moment, only if you make the right decision.

Unfortunately, for all of us, there is no right or wrong decision in the context of the universal mind. When you look at the world around you and realize that beyond the earth and into the darkness of space, you find that may not matter. However, the reality of our culture and the present life we live which includes the people we care about, it does in fact matter. If another person or group of people has made the wrong decision in life which has caused a chain of events, right or wrong, then you should, in fact, attempt to make it right. In the end, eventually the sun will die out, and the human race will have moved on. This future view of the world is sometimes necessary, as a majority of humans ignore the fact that they will have descendants who need to focus on these questions and find solutions to the problems we can't even imagine being faced with in our lifetime.

Year after year, we develop new ideas and new concepts because we are trying to find a way to complete the struggle, to get rid of the suffering in life by helping the homeless and the environment. We have a view that this is the way it is, but we have no choice as humans at this time, because of the actions that we have taken to not make a change. We are flawed and have to be a certain way; unfortunately, if we are no longer like this we won't be human, instead, we will be something else that may be along the lines of a technical nightmare. How can we remove what we are and be the same humans? If you try to fight what you are, then you will most likely not be the same person. In our era, technology has started to domesticate the human, making us lazy and giving us a false sense of control and security in our lives. For now, we may have the control we need with the contracts in our lives, but events that happen at this time period may cause major changes which are no longer in our control.

Since it is sometimes the case that the human has failed themselves, they turn to the law and government. The government is forcing existence for the future as we have created it to do so, sometimes being our failure. For this experience, and going beyond the normal intentions you cannot have multiple points of view, you must have a single one—you must make the sacrifice and go beyond, as this is the only time we get. Time is limited, and this is it, as we exist to understand these points of view and to be here now at this time. To the chain, you only have control over the paths that you have existence on, where your operational juncture is located.

It is also not about freedom, but the idea of being free. There will always be a person telling you what to do, forcing your opinion, but how you respond is up to you. We force each other's opinions at times, at the mercy of each other, and sometimes we realize how far we have gone and change our ways. This is the study of the universal mind and the study of the self, the will, as well as the survival instinct to move forward. It is those that prepare who move forward in continuing the species, to create a better tomorrow for those that may not have had one at all. There are only so many people that perform this act of personal development, and so few that will accept the truth of who they are as humans.

It is now the time to make an affirmation to go beyond the chaotic nature of the human without control. Take control of your life as it currently is, and move forward into a world of order. Think about where you would be if you had not made the proper decisions, the 'right' decisions that have made your life as unique as it is. We know that there is in fact order in chaos, a true nature to the system even if we don't fully understand it. That is the value of being human, accepting that beyond all negativity we exist as a species that continues to create no matter what the cost. The downside to this is that we look at some of our own as expendable, and in time we learn that with technology we can solve problems sometimes even before they occur.

PRACTICAL APPLICATIONS

In the end, after you have accepted your destiny of who you are as a person, you must be calm and at peace. It's at this point where you should be perfectly content with all of the knowledge you have obtained throughout your years on Earth, and be able to present the information in some manner that helps others achieve their goals. By this point in your cycle, you should be beyond creating a schedule for your daily life and have changes that would be fit for a master. Be whole with your theory and actions. Complete them in a way that makes you feel complete. If this is not yet the case, then one must keep moving forward through the struggle that is your world. As you develop your mind through the changes of time, you should know at this point, you will be able to push through the negativity and prepare accordingly for each potential situation.

The life you live should be an example for future generations, and essentially it will be your legacy; it is important that you live up to this as much as possible. As you make history in your journey, put forth your best interests on a daily basis by focusing on what makes the most sense, what is relevant to not only you but to others as well.

Actions and Thoughts:

- Accept who you are but move forward reasonably.

- Complete a personal symbolic representation of your life which can assist you in finding your true purpose.

- Mentor others in the duties of a human, and work to live up to a universal standard.

- Be fair in your actions, and always think of others as you would think of yourself.

- Always remember where you came from, but continue to move forward on your journey.

A lot of people jump to the ending.

This page is for those people.

If by chance you have jumped to the last page of this book in hopes of knowing the ending, then you have learned nothing. I know that with absolute certainty; life is about the destination but only through the correct path. Anybody can reach a point in their life and gain insight. However, who takes the correct path and, in the end, knows without a doubt that they led a life worth living?

Where do you want to be?

THE AUTHOR

Tom J. Limber is an expert in subjectivism and has a lifelong interest in knowledge-based philosophical frameworks and how when used properly they could possibly transcend the normal human experience to achieve a higher standard of living. Mr. Limber has a primary focus on existentialism and metaphysics, and his approach in this text builds on the ancient Buddhist teachings of the universal mind, and how science and philosophy are available to us as to examine ourselves and the modern-day activities that we perform.

Mr. Limber has over 10 years' experience as an IT Security Specialist and has worked as a Network Engineer at several companies when this time was directly impacted by "cyber" war that now exists in the world. Mr. Limber has completed his Master's Degree in Information Assurance and earned the following career certifications: **CISSP, CISA, CCNA, CCNP, ITIL v3, JNCIA-JUNOS, MCP, GIAC ISO 27001, CompTIA A+, Network+, Security+, and also the CEH and CHFI. Mr. Limber is certified with National Security Agency INFOSEC Certified NSTISSI No. 4011 and 4012.**

Printed in Great Britain
by Amazon

59794703R00108